ONWARD
TO
MANHOOD

"Mr. Eric Elliott is one of the best communicators through the use of the written and spoken language (English) that I've experienced in my lifetime. His book reveals biblical truths and challenges Christian men to reassess the way we are raising our sons/mentees to become godly men/husbands/fathers in our 21st century society. This book is a must read for especially Christian men; however, the benefits accrue to all men universally."

—**Pastor Walter Hamilton, III**, Christ Fellowship Church

Having read the book and knowing the character of the author, I am pleased to have the opportunity to provide this endorsement. I am an educator who has devoted my life's work to assisting and encouraging young people to become productive, educated individuals and contributors to a changing society.

I have known the author for more than two decades. Mr. Elliott was an undergraduate student at Old Dominion University. He was working as a tutor counselor. He demonstrated strong leadership skills, was an excellent mentor and role model for younger males and his peers. He was as genuine in his interactions with his mentees as he is with his readers in this book.

In Direction to a Place of Manhood, as a reader, I sense the genuiness he shares with his readers about his personal life experiences and lessons learned as a part of his plight to becoming a focused determined man; overcoming all barriers that sometimes handicap potential fathers, educators, men of God, good leaders and good citizens.

This is a book written for today's boys and men of all ages. Fathers, grandfathers, uncles and men action fellowship groups educate the male by using this great book as the direction to manhood.

—**Ollie W. Tolliver, Ed.S.**, Director, Upward Bound Program
Old Dominion University

Eric Elliott has communicated truths and remedies not revealed to him by flesh and blood! His insights connect with the true spiritual nature of men as purposed by our creator. A timely work for times such as these.

—**Pastor Paul S. Pleasants**, Calvary Baptist Church,
Christchurch, VA

This book is an inspirational training guide to transform immature young males to become magnificent productive men who choose to embrace godly principles and godly priorities. It is filled with wisdom ways for winning, formulas for fulfillment and strategies for success to enhance, enable and empower boys of blithe to become successful men of purpose. CHECK IT OUT!

—**Evangelist Dr. Christipher Joy,** Love Crusade Evangelistic Ministries, Rialto, CA

Sometimes a man has to go and find a place where he can be in great solitude so that he may ponder, hypothesize and find ways to bring those thoughts created in solitude to fruition for the good of the men amongst him. Eric Elliott has found such a place and his thoughts are as deep as the debts of one's soul. Excellent job with superbly flushed out thoughts for men who seek or need to seek God.

—**Anthony "Von" Mickle,** Author of *Slide 68: 86 Your Current Life and Pursue the Lifestyle You've Been Dreaming Of.*

Eric, I have been challenged, stirred and empowered to become a better man and to inspire others to do the same. Your book is necessary reading for all young men and women. I shared excerpts with my daughter and she is eager to read the entire book. Your treatise on manhood is simple yet profound. You are a modern day prophetic voice for the men of this age and the age to come. If we apply the wisdom of these pages, we can become shapers and designers of a better world.

—**Pastor Silas Oliver,** 21st Church of God

Bravo!!! This book is a much-needed reality check for manhood. The spiritually—rich chapters are a guiding MAN*call to action. As a woman, and mother of an adult son I had no idea the depth of maturity men must achieve to live a productive life. I believe this book will help men look in the mirror, while holding onto God's hand.*

—**Gail L. Lee,** Director of Development for The Children's Home, Baltimore, MD

Eric Elliott has written a thoughtful and provocative work sorely needed in the area of biblical manhood. ONWARD TO MANHOOD accurately identifies areas of manhood that many men often overlook because of unawareness or denial. Elliott's insightful analysis of the gulf between young boys and adult manhood reveals the invasive influence that individualism, social media, and misdirection exists to compromise their character and growth. He has a clear agenda. He wants faithful folk [boys and men] to become "unstuck" and move to new levels in their personal and spiritual lives. Simply put, this work is calling for us [men] to abandon every notion of mediocrity and access the excellence resident in all of us.

—Dr. **Nathaniel Brooks**, Youth & Young Adult Pastor, MT.

Pleasant Baptist Church, Herndon, VA

In this very timely book, Onward TO MANHOOD, Brother Eric has written a "must have" volume that should be in the hands of every person and/or organization that has an interest in the health and well-being of our young men of African descent. There is a plethora of instances which one could point to that remind us of the need to instill within our young men the need to have self-esteem and a healthy respect for those around them.

As African Americans, we are reminded almost daily of the fact that our very skin color is an affront to some in our society, and as a result we are always in a state of unease in what is supposed to be a free society. This volume is invaluable as we make concerted efforts to ensure that this, and generations to follow, will be positive contributors to our communities in particular and to our society in general.

I sincerely hope that this book will be widely accepted and read. After all, "IT'S AN AT-HOME PERSONAL WORKSHOP—MEANT TO BE READ, ABSORBED, AND ACTUALIZED." If the author's desires are realized, indeed, ours will be a better society in which to live.

—Rev. Dr. **Sylvester T. Smith**, Pastor, Good Shepherd Baptist Church

Assistant Professor of Ethics, Samuel

DeWitt Proctor School of Theology

Virginia Union University

ONWARD
TO
MANHOOD

ESTABLISHING GODLY MASCULINITY

ERIC ELLIOTT

Onward To Manhood

©2015 by Eric Elliott

Unless otherwise noted, scripture quotations are taken from *The Holy Bible, New International Version*® (NIV). Copyright © 1973, 1978, 1984, 2011 by Biblica, Inc.™ Used by permission of Zondervan. All rights reserved worldwide. www.zondervan.com. The "NIV" and "New International Version" are trademarks registered in the United States Patent and Trademark Office by Biblica, Inc.™

Scripture quotations identified as NLT are taken from the *Holy Bible*, New Living Translation, copyright ©1996, 2004, 2007 by Tyndale House Foundation. Used by permission of Tyndale House Publishers, Inc., Carol Stream, Illinois 60188. All rights reserved.

Scripture quotations identified ESV are from The Holy Bible, English Standard Version® (ESV®), copyright 2001 by Crossway, a publishing ministry of Good News Publishers. Used by permission. All rights reserved. ESV Text Edition: 2007.

Scripture quotations identified NKJ are taken from *The Holy Bible*, New King James Version. Copyright © 1979, 1980, 1982 by Thomas Nelson, Inc. Used by permission. All rights reserved.

Library of Congress Cataloging-in-Publication Data
Elliott, Eric
    Onward To Manhood: Establishing Godly Masculinity / Eric Elliott
p. cm.

ISBN: 978-1508950936

Printed in the United States of America
22 21 20 19 18 17 16 15   10 9 8 7 6 5 4 3 2 1

Design by Peter Gloege | LOOK Design Studio

Editorial development and creative design support by Ascent:
www.itsyourlifebethere.com

Follow Eric Elliott:

 OnwardToManhood   www.EricJElliott.com

This book is :

Dedicated to my bride Kimberly,
because I have found you (and continue to discover you)
I have found favor from the Lord. Your brilliance
is surpassed only by your beauty, inner & outer–
woooooooweeee, I am tremendously blessed.
I love and value you immensely!

Dedicated to Sophia – What a joy you are!

Dedicated, finally, to my son Ethan.
It's my desire that you experience,
exalt and extend God in such a way
that others want to do the same

This book was written,
in tribute to my father,
Meriman J. Elliott,
and my sons, Samuel Anthony
and Caleb Joshua Elliott ...
To eulogize a father and two sons requires
God's grace and raises lots of questions.
Their lives are dearly cherished and missed.

CONTENTS

"Our people must learn

to devote themselves to doing

what is good, in order that they

may provide for daily necessities

and not live unproductive lives."

Titus 3:14 (NIV)

PROLOGUE

Daily we are bombarded by wayward voices, full of dialogue but devoid of Godly direction. Internal and external pressures cause boys to grow up faster and experience things sooner than ever before. Without a foundation of timeless truth, life is chocked full of choking choices. Internet sites, cable channels, tabloids, magazines, satellite radio and television all vie for the attention (and money) of men, especially young men in the 14-34 age range. There are even political fronts, educational efforts, social programs and legislative movements purported to aid men, but they bring about their ruin. The many forces and faces that serve only to derail our lives from their intended excellence are closing in quickly, silently and surely.

Not only are external pressures causing boys to grow up faster and experience things sooner, internal stresses are as well. Many of us are missing the marks of manhood and others of us don't even know that such marks exist. While Amber Alerts notify us of missing children, there ought to be some amber alerts for the hallmarks missing from modern manhood. Hallmarks such as productivity, reverence, boldness, conviction, consideration, love, correct thinking and mandatory respect for women, continue to evaporate. A close look at families, neighborhoods and schools reveals a dire need for direction. This book was written to bolster boys and young men by giving Godly guidance as they mature to manhood. In addition, it gives insight and spiritual refreshment to the women who have become exhausted and exasperated with the men they are trying to understand.

Have you noticed the tsunami of apathy that has engulfed the youth of today? Many are hard to educate because they've never been taught the value of learning. Countless others won't receive discipline because they have never been taught its value. Some will curse everyone because they haven't been loved by anyone. Others don't show respect because they haven't seen it modeled.

Scores of young men are beat up, locked up or closed up in a coffin when they should be rising up in the relevance and power of God. Pathetic is the day when boys get locked up only to meet their father and uncles for the first time. If you are currently detained in jail, don't let that sentence write the final chapter of your life! The last time you stood before a judge, she said you would serve time. That day has passed and now it is your chance to make time serve you well. The determination of your soul dictates whether you serve time or time serves you. You are still the product of creative splendor. The Master's unmistakable fingerprints of glory are all over you!

INTRODUCTION TO THE ULTIMATE MAN

Every boy should become a man! There is no such thing as drifting into manhood; it is an intentional journey. Through repeated practical examples, this book offers hope as you navigate and negotiate your way into adulthood. Several years ago, Pastor Walter Hamilton III shared with his Sunday morning congregation, "Jesus is the Word that became flesh. As Christians we are flesh that should become more like the Word." Without an authentic relationship with God through His only begotten Son, Jesus, there are portions of this book that will make no sense and seem ridiculous.

Here is the foundational tenet of this book: God loves you and God created you; because of that, you have tremendous value. Upon this foundational statement we will build the case for manhood. Any teaching, doctrine or documentation that does not support this foundational statement will not and cannot give you a full view of your past, present or future. Without a full view, there can be no fulfillment. Here is the basis for this book.

1. God has a plan for your life. He cares about your life and has designed it on purpose and with reason. That reason is to advance His cause, since His cause leads to meaning.

2. God's plan gives meaning. Man was created to live a life of relevance. Our relevance gives us meaning and that meaning provides direction.

3. God's plan gives direction. Direction is the connection between today's action and tomorrow's accomplishment. It is the vital ingredient in a life of stability; that stability cultivates peace.

4. God's plan brings peace. Focus on Him fosters peace and minimizes self-centeredness. A life, a time, or a place of peace allows us to sense His presence and sync with His plan.

5. God's plan involves you, but is not all about you! His plan is for you to live with Him

in Heaven. Eventually, God wants to take us on an adventure reserved only for people spiritually alive in Him. Obviously that time has not yet come, so until then, refer to number 1 again.

If this five-point plan seems radical, it is because modern living encourages us to live sloppy lives with very little discipline or accountability. Psalm 62:11 (NLT) declares that power belongs to God; subsequently it comes from Him.

PREFACE

This book was born out of an obligation to share some of the blessed wisdom that has fueled my life.

My father once told me, '"Some people are wise and some people are otherwise." The voice of the 'otherwise' seem to pervade the airwaves. No doubt, there will be sections of this book that you will not agree with; feel free to disagree. In all of print, there are only 66 indisputable books; this ain't one of them! If you agreed with everything in this book, it would not be necessary to read or write it. This publication will ruffle your feathers while putting wind beneath your wings. Throughout this print, I have painted pictures so that reading this book equates to watching a movie. I encourage you to read this book with a pen in hand as you will find several places to script and co-produce this blockbuster film called 'Your Life.' To each reader, 'Your Life' is the number one box office drama to hit the big screen. Places everyone!! The stage is set and the curtains have been drawn for 'Your Life'—Action!!!

CHAPTER ONE

AFFINITY
STATEMENT

Recently I worked a stint at a well-known upscale clothier. One of my customers came in looking for small and extra small clothes. He had lost thirty pounds as a result of an addiction to a prescription drug. Candidly, he told me about his time in rehab and his determination to not experience that ever again. I listened intently as he bared his soul. His experience explained why his 5'10" and 130lb frame required kid-sized clothing. As a retail seller, I could attire his frame but do nothing to address his soul.

My customer's choices had taken him to death's door and now he was grappling to find his way to a more respectable path in life. Without God's grace and the examples of reputable men, I might have stumbled along a similar path.

Several unforgettable turning points mark my path to manhood.

At the age of seven, my 2nd grade teacher, Mrs. Morisson said to me, "You have great potential." I didn't really know what potential was but it sounded like something decent. My dad often reminded me of her words.

Not every influence I came across was as helpful. A childhood acquaintance, Patrick, repeatedly told me, "Your daddy looks like a monkey." This deeply damaging comment took me down a rung or two in my growth. I now realize that Patrick probably felt like garbage, so he wanted to impose his trashy life on others.

There were also aimless men who turned freeloading into a sport. Topping that list was one of my aunt's boyfriends who believed he did not need to work because, in his words, "God would provide." I didn't know him that well, but it was evident that he was a bona fide loafer who just wanted to get over. His example helped me quickly identify what it looked like to have a boy's belief and a man's body.

As I got older, it became apparent to me that I needed more positive guides. During my freshman year of college I met Virgil, who was a junior in mechanical engineering.

He became a mentor and his guidance was crucial to me during my first two years of college. Countless times, he inquired about my classes, remembered when I had tests, reminded me of them, and then asked how I did on them. Unwittingly, he taught me to concern myself with others.

Not only was I affected by relationships, there were times that shaped my life as well.

The most solemn time in life was my dad's death. For decades I watched him serve as a stabilizing force in the lives of others. When my aunt and uncle struggled with alcoholism and emotional instability, Dad responded by housing my cousin for a couple of years. When he got tired of seeing his mother live in public housing, Dad purchased a home for her. He always bolstered when others faltered. He was a pillar, and after his death, I made a choice.

I decided to carry his example forward.

Marriage was also a defining moment. Saying "I do" was a piece of cake. I clearly remember returning home from our beach honeymoon, one of my first questions to my new bride was, "What am I supposed to do with you now?" One of her first orders of business was rearranging my apartment. My posters of Michael Jordan and Charles Barkley were nixed and all photo albums containing pictures of other women were deep sixed.

Sixteen years later, I contend that marriage is the most acute test of manhood. It has compelled me to become a man that my wife could be proud to call her husband. Everyday marriage propels me onward to manhood.

Perhaps the most poignant moment occurred around age 27 when my much younger cousin saw me shaving. With innocent bewilderment, he asked what I was doing. It stood to reason that without a father present he was not familiar with the shaving process. I explained to him the what and why of shaving. Fast forward ten years later when I introduced my own son to shaving. I often 'shaved' my ticklish son with my electric razor, blade cover in place, as he giggled during the whole experience. We stood face to face in the mirror as shaving partners. He looked in the mirror and saw his future while I looked in that same mirror and saw my past. In just a whiff of time, he'll experience that same nostalgia.

The watershed moment was the birth of my first two children Sophia and Ethan! Holding a totally dependent newborn deepened my appreciation for the miracle of birth and life. I recall holding my newborns and thinking, we all start this way. In order to reach adulthood, a lot has to go right. I pray God gives me the grace to raise my children and turn those watershed moments into lives well-lived.

Undoubtedly, the most sobering time of fatherhood was the death of my two sons, Samuel and then one year later, Caleb. When we received news that my wife was expecting our third child, there was no way to predict what was about to befall us. My wife's pregnancy with Sammy was relatively smooth, the calm before the storm. Caleb's was a painful and problematic pregnancy. Both wound up at Reston Hospital as distressed deliveries. Sammy was delivered at 1.1 pounds and Caleb's weight hardly registered. Neither child survived. What an empty feeling to leave the maternity ward with no newborn buckled into the baby seat. While others left the neonatal unit with their new arrival, we exited empty handed. Twice our pregnancy celebration turned to lamentation.

In that obstetrics ward, the most chilling moment of my life occurred as I gazed upon my stillborn son. Although I felt like hiding, there was nowhere to go. There we were, face to face with my son's lifeless body, a frozen future. My wife was totally spent; I felt useless and helpless. I had faith in God as the Healer, but for this moment, I called and got a busy signal. Seeing my wife in such emotional drain, physical pain and spiritual disdain left me in my most inept moments ever as a husband.

At the memorial service, Samuel Anthony Elliott's

miniscule body lay in a football-sized cooler on top of a wobbly table. We left that cemetery as a shell of ourselves and I've since concluded that no parent should have to bury their child. For my third son, the saga was even more sorrowful. What the hospital labeled as "medical waste" was a fetus who bore my surname—Caleb Josiah Elliott.

Here's the burden I bore, I had idealized fathering a family of two sons and a daughter. My motive sprang out of growing up in Richmond, VA, where during my adolescence black males had a 1 in 21 chance of being murdered. In my own noble but naïve way, I desired to father just two boys who would begin to reverse the stereotype of 'no good men' and become outstanding men, husbands and fathers.

To this day, I miss having those two extra sons to raise and wrestle. Those losses gave me a greater appreciation for my living children. As a result, I value laughter and time with my kids. I see two empty seats at my dining room table where two children should be. We have Christmas stockings for both Samuel and Caleb. They serve as memorials to two family members who did not live beyond the maternity ward. Both of these episodes left me in a grieved state, yet I discerned God's bottomless love for me.

While these losses left me in the grip of sadness and pain, they taught me to cry out to God for help, strength and answers. As His presence eventually filled those two deep holes in my soul, it was as if He allowed those depths to be bored into me so that He could form pillars of spiritual "granite", so to speak, making me a stronger man than I had been before.

As time passed, a new strength carried me forward. It lifted me to a place where I could praise God for unveiling his grace and goodness to escort me through life's dismal times. The strength gained from these losses, far surpassed anything gained by sitting in a Sunday service, reading a book or attending a weekend conference.

A PLACE CALLED MANHOOD

I was blessed to be guided into manhood by some great mentors. For that reason, it's time to pay that great gift forward. A Swedish proverb says, "The afternoon knows what the morning never suspected." Since I am in the afternoon of life, this book is commissioned to skillfully chaperone those in the a.m. (amateur man) into your p.m. (professional man). Without that essential escort, young men have begun to dance with a dubious list of pathetic partners. Included on the list of cohorts are the: confused, wimpy, lazy, abusive, elusive, predatory, sexually immoral, sneaky, mean, murderous, hateful and resentful. Every man has entertained at least one partner on this list. The longer we dance with that partner, the more we *become* that partner.

Because of the strong and lasting 'menfluences' in my life, I was spared from the marginal subsistence offered by selfishness and apathy. From their examples, I have learned to date my daughter, listen to my wife, take my son on outings, and persevere in marriage. Furthermore, their teachings have sustained me during personal times of rebellious and hedonistic living.

The sum total of these dealings with men can be attributed to selected highlights. Both high school and college graduation are the byproducts of their inspiration. Those feats led to higher aspirations such as national oratorical contests, company acknowledgements, as well as invitations to speak at jails, colleges, churches and corporations. Especially meaningful have been fatherly recognitions and special cards written to me by my wife. All of this was made possible by the grace of God and following men on meaningful paths.

This book lyrically forges that same path for you! On this path, the reader will embrace industry, social consciousness, interdependence, faith and fun. Additionally, it will help punch your ticket to academic advancement, community involvement, spiritual fulfillment, physical development, and financial empowerment. This leads to a loving concern for wife or girlfriend, authentic manhood and fatherhood. This declaration is designed to give each reader an awareness of his significance. Here's to a hope infusion for all who read this book. I pray that this marks the return of prominent men!

CHAPTER TWO

WHERE IS THE MANual?!

CHECK OUT THIS CHAPTER

God defines a man and then man
defines culture. Anytime that order is inverted,
the definition of a man is perverted.

Decisions are the dividing line between
a life of trifle and one of significance.

This book will escort you to the realm
of significant manhood where men bear a
strong family likeness to Jesus Christ.

INFORMATION IS ABUNDANT BUT DIRECTION IS PRICELESS.

Not long ago, we ordered our first smartphones. The arriving package included the phone, accessories, a Start Guide, and Warranty Information. Surprisingly, the warranty information contained more details than the Start Guide.

Some of the uses of this new device were intuitive, but many were not. In the process of looking for a way to change the data settings and download applications, I got totally lost. Caught up in new-toy-excitement, I had not thought about a manual. When I discovered that I could not set up my device properly, I started looking for one. There was none to be found.

Not one to harbor questions, I called my cell phone carrier and they offered to send me a copy of a manual. Smartphones had been on the market for over a decade before we decided to get one. Evidently that was long enough for most users to learn how to maneuver one without the use of a guidebook. Typically, I would ignore the included manuals for items we purchased such as the kids' toys or a bookshelf, instinctively knowing how to put them together. Manipulating a smartphone presented a stiffer challenge.

Is the message: what the product does is more important than how to effectively use it? Perhaps the message is: we know you'll figure out how to use it because it's been on the market for more than a decade. Maybe the idea is to call the carrier with questions so they can sell more services and plans. Perhaps the marketing team concluded that no one has time to read the all-important write-up. Possibly, it was cost prohibitive to produce written manuals. Whatever the reason was, it left me unprepared to command the tool in my hands. In just a matter of a few frustrating moments, I concluded: For such a valuable tool, the manual ought to be included.

This techno-encounter is symbolic of the transition many of us make from boyhood to manhood. When we face new and daunting situations, we usually look for some point of reference. Too often, when questions arise, we rely on bad experiences or insufficient information in order to navigate to a solution. Without proven parameters, the choices we make can be misguided, ill-advised or even ruinous. This is the day of unlimited choices, whether we are talking cereals, channels, restaurants, colleges, pizza or women. Wherever there are unlimited choices, there's a dire need for sage voices.

In the cyberworld, there is an app for just about anything, whether it's choosing a tie, friends, a car, a lawnmower or training for a 5K race. In a literal sense, there are dozens of apps for each of these 'choices'. Cyber choices don't usually have the same implications as 'real' choices. How do we begin to narrow down the choices and pinpoint what's best for us? Having a manual opens up realms of possibility for the use of the product. Likewise, having a clear manhood objective gives us a life directive, maximizes our moments, increases our impact and amplifies our existence.

Messages contained herein embrace three circles of men. Circle one contains the likes of my childhood acquaintance, Mike. Mike had no detectable male presence in his life and was raised by his grandmother. Eventually he got connected with my mom's church, but still he wandered aimlessly through life. That directionless living resulted in a jail stint, which ironically was his only source of stability. Circle two consists of conscientious men who bear a sense of discontent with a job or career that is too inadequate to address the most compelling needs of family and community. Circle three includes the high achievers who eventually realize that life transcends affluence.

For years society has proffered imprecise definitions of manhood. However, manhood does not hinge on the accumulation of accolades, muscle capacity, titles, a portfolio, sexual prowess or number of children. Nor does it involve the perpetuation of crimes, developing street cred, racking up years of existence or achieving a level of fitness. God affirms that manhood emerges from a boy or man's continual, deliberate application of mental, physical, social and spiritual virtues. God defines a man, and then man defines culture. Anytime that order is inverted, the definition of a man is perverted; culture and society then artificially prop themselves up with wacky and whimsical definitions of manhood. They play out in numerous scenarios.

THE CAUTIONARY TALES OF MESSED UP MALES

I have observed and studied the lives of triumphant men, abysmal men and everything in between. Although my Uncle J. was a lamentable specimen, I learned a great deal from him. If meanness and muscle defined masculinity, he was *the man*. Legend has it that when he played football, he flattened folk on the gridiron and just left them there. It seemed like that was his only real feat in life. For years, he struggled with alcohol addiction. He was infamous for having a month long marriage. Repeatedly, his life was rubbed raw on the rugged edge of reality. Over time, he succumbed to the streets of Miami, liquor and hard living. Because of this wretched example, I avoided alcohol like rotten cabbage. From him I learned about toughness and street smarts. I also learned that I had a choice about what substances to put in my body. In my exposure to drugs and alcohol, I could not acquire a taste for them. I think that was God's sure way of limiting my foolish youthful antics.

As I reached my thirties, there were other men who negatively impacted me. Two nefarious instances come to mind. Richard Strong and Bruce Sands both set up investment fronts, enticing hundreds to participate in capital gains. In time, they accumulated millions of dollars. Those equities came about because they defrauded hundreds of people out of their personal finances. To their detriment, they were enamored with the lure of shiny cars, large bank accounts and a plentiful portfolio. We often pursue and acquire these effects, only to discover that these items cannot scratch our most profound itch. Our best offerings come from our core, the place where the hurt is the deepest and the love is most compelling. Because of our superficial orientation, we tend to envy the guy who has the biggest house, shiniest rims and most pronounced biceps. These are publicity- hungry times; hundreds of examples of men qualify for headlines, but few of them are remarkable as storylines.

THE INNER JOURNEY

Decisions are the dividing line between a life of trifle and significance. Every decision moves us closer to a desired end or a dead end. A short time ago, my co-worker told me that she had been working 46 years and had no real goals. Her objective had devolved into: go to work, collect the check and go home. She had no aspirations beyond that because the gusto had been slowly drained from her soul. She had been running the dead-end-treadmill of work to wage to weekend repeated to the point of exhaustion. She had yielded to a non-dynamic, dead-end decision. For a while, I floundered in that same fatalistic phase. You can see that same futility in the eyes of lots of guys. The default level of men who abandon decision making is no goals and low gusto.

The difference between trifling men and significant men lies in the comparison between a cruise ship and a battle ship. Anticipating nothing short of a good time, people book a cruise. Many guys conduct their days as if they have set sail for a series of pleasure destinations; seeking solely to satisfy themselves. Cruise ship commuters are all about maximizing the time spent in entertainment, enjoyment and consumption. They pay for the option of endless recreation, dining, relaxing, socializing and sight-seeing. An overwhelming fun factor anesthetizes the mind. The love of games, girls and gambling is so hypnotic that little else can register. Anything with thoughtful overtones is seen as mental strain and not agenda-worthy. Likewise the trifling man designates his days primarily for good times, luxuries and indulgences. All memorable cruises set sail for pleasure destinations but ultimately return to everyday reality.

On a battle ship, it's all about being prepared to execute a mission. Each member of that craft has an assignment which ties into a larger objective. Without a mission, there is no reason to serve anything greater than self. Having spent time in boot camp and preparation, these men are equipped and dispatched to confront adverse conditions. They are all qualified and endorsed, aware that the mission is not about them. Having been briefed by an authority, those on a battle ship move purposefully toward a designated target. They occupy a given region, ready to respond to circumstances. Every man is vetted and commissioned for his station.

Both cruise ships and battle ships have occasions to drop anchor, but for very different reasons. The anchor question here for you is: Does your life bear more resemblance to the cruise ship or the battle ship?

This book will introduce you to four quadrants of masculinity. Quadrants are really a frame of mind. Quadrant one is the home of immaturity. In this place you might find a kid climbing on a counter to get a scoop of sugar and in the process, makes a mess. He could be totally surrounded by the mess he made and be oblivious to it or not know how to clean it up. He then promptly walks away from it. That same kid could find himself living in his parent's basement 30 years later with no real ambition in life. In Q1, boys are *callous or curious enough* to create problems.

Quadrant two houses the inquisitive type. Here young men are keen enough to ask questions. It may come in the form of "why do I have to do what you say?" That question could be the sincere reflection of someone seeking the security of boundaries or it could have a rebellious slant. In Q2, young men are *keen enough* to ask questions.

Quadrant three accommodates the seasoned guys. When 'life staple' questions arise such as 'what am I going to do with my life?' they, like the rest of us, feel overwhelmed or scared witless. All the while they have some form of an answer. In Q3, maturing men are *aware enough* to seek answers to questions.

Quadrant four is outfitted with case studies of sturdy men. These are the guys who, if they don't have the money to fund a project, can bankroll it with ideas, inspiration or elbow grease. Even if they have no clue how to conclude a matter, they continue to walk in faith toward the finish line. In Q4, we find men who are *stout enough* to provide solutions. Every man should dare to reach up to a man in the 'next' quadrant while reaching out to a man in a previous quadrant.

This book will escort you to the realm of significant manhood where men bear a strong family likeness to Jesus Christ. My hope is that after reading this book you will be able to paint a vivid picture of a significant man, with your face clearly posted! Your future is calling; let the significant man answer.

CHAPTER THREE

THE MANhunt STARTS NOW!

You are defined by Divine design!

The man who pays too much attention to trivial things, will begin to feel insignificant. A man who feels insignificant long enough, begins to feel irrelevant and is very easily wiped out.

You become a man in order to be manhandled, like it or not. Along the way, you will endure the misunderstanding and ridicule of those who stand to benefit the most from your transformation into manhood.

YOUR ASSIGNMENT DEMANDS FULFILLMENT.

Sports represented a skill set to which most of my peers could relate. Many of my friends had dreams of playing professional sports. I too had those fleeting thoughts, but those lofty dreams were dipped in sobriety. As a sought after track athlete, a proficient basketball player and a marginal football player, I had little desire to pursue those sports as a profession. For a while they were a passion and pastime.

As a preteen, the only reading I really wanted to do involved sports-related articles. Before there was any such thing as an internet search engine, I gathered data on top teams, elite players and their performances. I pored through the local sports pages and publications such as Basketball Digest, The Sporting News, Street & Smith's, Sports Illustrated, etc. Staying current on my favorite athletes such as Julius Erving, Edwin Moses, Evelyn Ashford and Tony Dorsett; gave me plenty to talk about. I would memorize basketball and football statistics in order to verbally spar against my friends who had also memorized stats about their favorite teams and players. These disputes took place at the middle school lunch table where everyone was an articulate advocate for his favorite sports teams.

Because of my intense study of these sports periodicals, my dad often declared that I would be a straight 'A' student if I studied my academic subjects the same way I studied the sports page. Rarely was there a grading period when I was in danger of making straight 'As'. Just as I rifled voraciously through numerous sports articles, men today are also searching. Our search extends beyond the exploration of articles and television channels to a level of yearning. This is the quest in Quadrant 1 of the manhood expedition. It is a yearning to discover identity, develop personae, and actualize achievement. Author John Eldridge gives a 'spot-on' assessment when he describes men as 'Wild at Heart'. We seek times that are action-packed, adventure-filled and aggression-laced. Because we are wired for conquest, we are always looking for a contest. The athletic, pornographic, entertainment, gambling and gaming industries continue to thrive because they give pseudo-satisfaction to this basic desire. These industries are fueled by billions of dollars especially among 18-40 year old men. In addition, they each allow a momentary escape from the daily load of living by temporarily numbing the mind. Too many of us halt our search at this futile level.

The man who pays too much attention to trivial things, will begin to feel insignificant. A man who feels insignificant long enough dons irrelevance and is very easily wiped out. Manhunts which float along a pointless path result in squandered existence. It is in a deeper pursuit, that a man finds his meaning. To the world, finding meaning is not important because it does not fit the profile of the superficial or shallow. Beyond the memories of glory days or momentary pleasures lies an organic layer of resolution. It is the resolve to contribute and become something meaningful. For most of us it is gradually released, based on where we invest time, talents, treasure and talk. Without cultivating meaning, we are easily swayed by what we see. We are provided no specific direction but pursue several. The progression from gangly male to developed man is necessarily rigorous.

Several men including my father helped me get my manhunt underway.

He often told me, "Son, what you want to be is an asset to society, not a liability." Coach Pleasants emphasized teamwork and passion on the basketball court.

On a team with college-level talent, he didn't allow any of us to become conceited. As a scout leader, Mr. Benjamin taught me about serving in the community. Uncle Norman showed me how to take enjoying life and socializing to the next level. To this day, I take note of his engaging people skills. Pastor Nichols exhibited exceptional responsibility and leadership. Twenty-five years after his death, I still give detailed attention to my spiritual growth. Grandpa Dorse stretched all of his resources because he made a meager subsistence, while Mr. Hyatt didn't mind showing us a good time through ample cash flow. Those men gave me the foundation for being grounded, grateful and gregarious. These images of men were seared into my pre-teen brain. It is because of these and others that I became conscious of possibilities and alive to opportunity.

In contrast, not all the guys I observed set noteworthy examples. Our next door neighbor Mr. Theron, was accused of breaking and entering into our home while we were on vacation. At that time in my life, all I really cared about was the condition of my 'Steve Austin' lunch box. Mr. Jones was a glowing example of irresponsibility; his sons were unruly and he was a father in absentia.

What makes the hunt so important? During the MANhunt, men 'find' themselves. People who don't find themselves or find their way, often find themselves wondering. Caught in a swirl of confusion, their recurring questions resemble the following: Why is life so hard? Why am I always jerked around? Why do I keep doing dumb stuff? Why have I plateaued at mediocrity? Those are the despondent questions that keep guys stuck in Quadrant 1. It's damnable to stay lost in boyhood one day beyond what is necessary. You are defined by Divine design! In God, every man has an assignment. We are all specially outfitted for an assignment

There is great value in the manhunt; it unleashes a

man's paramount questions. Several primary questions simmer in our souls: What should I be doing? What's my life all about? Is there more to life than this? What's my agenda? Several years ago, my then pastor, Enoch Butler lamented in conversation," Most men don't know what they are doing." In stark contrast, during the Colonial era, men in America were defined by fatherhood and community involvement. Marriage and fatherhood were among the highest priorities primarily because men realized their true vitality and impact as progenitors of society.

Nowadays the emphasis has shifted to a more detached, self-centered approach with a heavy accent on entertainment and minimal responsibility. Consequently we are portrayed as imbecilic and severely lacking in self-control, intelligence and leadership. During prime-time television broadcasts, this unflattering portrayal is repeated. We see characters who are pitiable and irrelevant, upheld as models for us to mimic. Adopting these portrayals has assisted in manhood sabotage. To further perpetuate the pathetic stream of behavior, entire channels and news publications are devoted to celebrity dating patterns, sports world stars' escapades, lascivious music videos, political mud-slinging and numerous other non-redeeming particulars. The constant coverage of infamous people who offer few redemptive qualities has plagued us so long that many men now take their life cues from them. There are numerous agents that obscure who you were created to be, many unknowingly. The longer this captivates our attention and dominates the headlines, the longer we will be distracted from our true worth

A truly advantageous manhunt involves other respectable men. Financial guru Dave Ramsey once said, "You never find successful people who do life alone." In every fruitful hunt, collaboration is crucial. Benefits of conducting a complete manhunt include: a reduction in the number of men involved in depression, suicides, homicides, murder-suicides, walking out, rapes, robberies, shooting rampages, pornography, etc. All of which reveal a manhunt gone awry. We are aware of Amber Alerts for lost or abducted children, there ought to be an Amber Alert for men who have lost their way. Such an 'Amber Alert' exists where men are socially connected—more on this in the chapter "Growth MANageMENt." Communities, states and nations will locate lost men when this Amber Alert is broadcast.

Every true hunt has at least one declared goal which defines the hunt itself. When that goal is obtained, the hunt is declared a success. The goal of a police manhunt is to find the person(s) responsible for a wrongdoing. What is the goal of your personal manhunt? Similar to that of law enforcement, it's essential to locate your *responsible* (inner) person. Even if you currently are not one, I know you have one! He may be hidden under years of discouragement, negligence or defeated living. I submit that the goal here is to be certain that you are on the path to manhood. Those who stray from the path usually do so because of damaging influences or circumstances. If you fail to take command of your situation, your situation will take command of you. What are you becoming? Carefully review the activities, events and happenings in your life over the past two months. They indicate what you are becoming. You become a man in order to be manhandled whether you want to or not. Along the way you will endure the ridicule of those who stand to benefit the most from your transformation. Become a man anyway!

Manhood is an exclusive pursuit, and its distinct sexual characteristics cannot be muddled with new-school ambiguous groups like agender, intersex, pangender, binary, etc. Identity clarity is the basic building block of manhood. Coupled with 'path certainty', the reader must answer the questions. What am I becoming? How successful has my manhunt been? How do I measure that success? By leaving these personal questions unanswered, you are destined for open-ended dysfunction.

Certainty is the hallmark of a man, necessary to exit Quadrant 1. There is something compelling about the man who has found his way and secured his direction. Have you ever noticed the demand for a caterer, mechanic, company president or personal trainer who shines with certainty? People will wait in line for their services because they are confident in the outcome they will provide. Get your manhunt started today.

CHAPTER FOUR

MANIPULATION
AND
woMANIPULATION

—————— **CHAPTER HIGHLIGHTS** ——————

"As a woman, she thinks that showing a little
skin will get her a little attention. As a man,
you think that what she is willing to show,
she is willing to share" —CREFLO DOLLAR

The enemy wants to take your sex drive
for a test drive and perform a drive-by on
your character while your life passes by.

"Since they call you a dog, this is one time
when you can act like a dog—they don't
just jump right in and jump right on-dogs
stop and sniff." —LANCE WATSON

Testosterone begins with t-e-s-t and ends with
o-n-e. Brothers, that's a clue to you—after you
pass the *test*, another *one* is on the way.

My desire is that both you and I develop a
relationship so honorable in the sight of the
Lord that others see it and abandon less
honorable ones in favor of ones like ours.

Increased sexual immorality will increase
the likelihood of your mortality.

What some call sexual healing
is really sexual stealing!

As long as you have libido plus any one of
the five senses, you WILL HAVE to address
the excitement and enticement of women.

Either we will stop the mess or
the mess will stop us.

Sony's Playstation has been one of the hottest selling items of this century! This dynamic entertainment system allows its users to simulate reality in an electronic gaming environment. Playstation, is a compound word consisting of two words—play and station. These two words are comprised of three word sounds: play, stay and shun. Interestingly enough these three word sounds are also the three options we have as it relates to the hottest topic in our life—women. When it comes to women, every one of us makes a daily decision to play, stay or shun. Whichever option we choose, increasingly it seems that the decision is based on her sexual accessibility. Using this play-stay-shun approach keeps us locked in gaming mode where we are always looking for different players, better versions and a higher score.

Each year the most popular video games are upgraded and given new wrinkles. Carrying that same gamesmanship into our relationship leads us to a place where we forget to value women. Instead we select what kind of genital joys they can provide. Conquest becomes the reason for the liaison and meaningful conversation is an afterthought. With every new relationship, the enemy wants to take your sex drive for a test drive. In doing so, he performs a drive-by on your character as your life passes by. How many drive-bys can you survive? Write that number here___. If that number is greater than zero, do you *really* want to find out?

Womanipulation occurs whenever a man's genitals become disconnected from his soul and guides him into pleasures without boundaries. It's this guy-notion which blossoms from the belief that sex is the sole goal. In this hypnotic state, he will gladly fixate on her behind and totally ignore her mind. Womanipulation will attenuate your courage, causing stunted spiritual, professional and emotional development. As more men are stricken with womaninpulation, an unintended yet massive spiritual hijacking takes place. The line-up of hijackers ranges from sexual harassment, STDs, unwanted pregnancies, pornography, prostitution and sexual assaults to name a few.

In the state of Womanipulation, the number one mode of transportation is lust. Renowned singer Marvin Gaye crooned a song about the capital city of Womanipulation, he called that place 'Sexual Healing'. In this capital city, it is legal to speed through emotional caution lights and ignore relational red lights in order to get to that sensual hot spot downtown called Sexual Healing. The prospect of visiting Sexual Healing has become so hypnotic that some guys will ignore all traffic signs, detours, delays and locked doors to get there. What some call sexual healing is really sexual stealing.

The surrounding suburbs of the capital city of Sexual Healing include Notion, Nurture, Nuptial, Not at All and Nub. In the neighborhood called Notion, the male residents are thinking about or starting to build up the courage to initiate a relationship but never quite get there.

In the community called Not At All, the residents opt for non-attachment and enjoy being all by themselves.

In the distant District of Nub, guy and girl meet up, sparks fly, but soon things begin to fizzle.

In the zone called Nurture, a man and a woman have developed chemistry and over time they begin to grow together. In the vicinity called Nuptial, couples have invested time into their love and look forward to solidifying a lifetime of devotion. We critically miss relational growth opportunities by taking the expressway straight to the capitol city.

IT STARTS WITH A GLANCE

We are all created in God's image, but the truth is images have a lasting influence over us. Any girl or woman whose image matches your preferred personal portrait will likely be highly attractive to you. In the beginning you see the 'video vixen' and are smitten! Sometimes women dress to get your attention. As a woman, she thinks that showing some skin will get her noticed. Pastor Creflo Dollar said, "As a man, you think that what she is willing to show, she is willing to share." In just a matter of minutes unbridled thoughts can race from 'Hi' to Let's get it on'. By taking the purely sexual path, the future is foreboding. You may have to deal with embarrassing tests for sexually transmitted diseases, expensive doctor's appointments, baby mama drama and legal proceedings as well as babies who are loud and awake when you want it quiet for sleeping. It's at this moment you realize that not every woman with an attractive face and shapely hips qualifies for your consideration, nor does she necessarily want it.

Womanipulation is much more than a scenario of two

independent bodies swapping body fluids. An entire plot is unfolding. It's almost as if the two souls are magnetically pulled into a lifelong drama, leaving behind a trail of mingled and mangled memories. The spark plug for it all is testosterone. Testosterone is that naturally occurring hormone which commands muscularity, sperm health and libido. Testosterone begins with t-e-s-t and ends with o-n-e. That's a clue to you—after you pass the test, another one is on the way. For boys, testosterone means unrestrained sexual energy without the benefit of boundaries provided by intellect or truthful consideration. So many times, it has unfolded like this:

HE LEFT, SO SHE'S LEFT...

He left in a hurry; now she's left hurting.

He left with a smile, but she's left with HPV.

He left with a maybe, and she's left with a baby!

He left to tell his friends;
now she's left with a bad reputation.

He left from the 2nd story window;
she's left with an unforgettable story.

He left to conquer another city;
she's left with her world shaken up.

He left relieved; she's left to re-live
the question—'What have I done?'

He left, knowing Victoria's Secret
and she's left with another dark secret.

He left, knowing how *to get her*,
she's left wondering—'Will we ever truly be *together*?'

He left never to look back,
she's left with destructive thoughts in the back of her mind.

He left thinking—'She'd better not be pregnant'!
she's left wondering—'What kind of daddy might he be?'

Although the experience feels good, there is a price to pay. In your wake, there's likely a trail of women with jolted emotions. Before you get her alone, get alone with yourself. Ask yourself—'Do I really care about her (spirit, soul and body) or do I just want to enjoy her body?

THE PROPOSITION THAT THE OPPOSITION DOESN'T WANT YOU TO ADOPT!

If you haven't disagreed with anything in the previous chapters, this will likely be the place of dissent. For years, the 'Safe sex' ideology has been touted as a way to slow the spread of sexually transmitted diseases and unwanted pregnancies. Certainly it's a better alternative than rampant ignorance, unchecked disease and pandemic problems.

The two paramount questions no one seems to be asking are: "Do we want to slow the disease or stop the disease?" and "Do we want to decrease our chances for Sexually Transmitted Diseases or eliminate them?" This is one time when you'd rather be part of the 'have nots' than the 'haves'. I challenge you to find out why your opinion about safe sex is so embedded in your psyche. There is a huge difference (and thriving economy) in slowing versus stopping STDs. When we truly believe a warning, it influences our behavior.

Consider this illustration on the difference between slowing and stopping. A young driver was speeding through a residential neighborhood. An officer pulled him over for failing to come to a complete stop at a stop sign. The boy pleaded his case by saying to the officer, "I saw the stop sign, and I slowed down enough to make sure no traffic or pedestrians were around. When I saw that the way was clear, I continued on my way. The officer replied, "Young man, the reason I pulled you over is that you failed to come to a complete stop at the stop sign." Fearing that the officer would not see things his way, the boy tried to cleverly ease his way out of a ticket. The boy said, 'Stop or slow down, what's the big deal??" The officer then took out his nightstick and began to lightly rap on the boy's head. He then asked the driver, "Would you like me to stop or to slow down?"

Brothers, the nightstick called 'STD' is literally and figuratively rapping us on the head. If we choose not to stop it, it will stop us. Satan wants to see the sexuality of every boy and man in SKIDD status. That is where he steals, kills, destroys or distorts our sexuality. Sexuality is *stolen* when a boy or man encounters incest, rape or molestation. Authentic male sexuality is *killed* when it manifests feminine traits or adopts homosexual tendencies. Sexuality is destroyed when racked by venereal disease. Sexuality is distorted when its appetite is perverted through pornography.

Let's face it. We want to cleverly rationalize our actions, then actualize our feelings. As long as we have libido and any one of the five senses, we will have to deal with the excitement and enticement of women. Pastor Anthony Francis encouraged us to, "Ask yourself the question. What story do I want to tell?"

Is it one of shame, regret or braggadocios conquest?

Do you want to confess to God that your previous relationship was a devious relationship? Dr. Nathaniel Brooks once pronounced, "If you don't want the memory, then don't do the deed." Recognize that sex was originally meant to be a benefit of a monogamous marital relationship. Sex is a puzzle piece and without God's big picture we have no idea where it fits in.

WHEN HORMONES WON'T LEAVE US ALONE

I remember that pivotal day when I finally called a stop to premarital sex. It was a moment of truth the day I wrote, "Thank God for small victories" in the margin of my bible. By His Holy Spirit, I finally experienced and understood what it meant to be liberated from the bondage of fornication. If sex opens the door to a relationship, it will slam the door on that same relationship. It fogs the decision-making process by replacing true intimacy with a surge of intensity. That intensity comes about because sex is a wondrous network of bonding physically, spiritually and emotionally. Experienced repeatedly, it creates physio-mental dependency in the brain similar to that of a habitual drug user.

Is there an escape from womanipulation? Yes! Here's how to resist enticements that may lead to entrapment. First, stop and sniff—Pastor Lance Watson gave a brilliant analogy between man and canine when he compared a dog in heat to a sexually excited male. He said, "Brothers, since they often call you a dog, this is the one time where you can act like a dog. Before one dog mates with another, it stops long enough to sniff. Sniffing allows the dog to collect vital information about where his mate has been previously. They don't jump right in and jump right on, dogs sniff." Stop and sniff give God time to step in. Have you stopped long enough to collect some vital information? For instance, are you sure the girl you are about to kiss, has been a girl all of her life or is this a recent development? What is her level of emotional stability?

Secondly, differentiate between love and lust. Dr. Martin Luther King Jr said, "The highest form of maturity is self-evaluation." Evaluate yourself on the love vs. lust continuum. Lust and love are comparable passions pointed in different directions. Lust seeks to immediately satisfy and love seeks to continually edify. Protracted lust is a huge impediment to long term thinking. A marriage conference speaker once grabbed the attention of all those contemplating marriage by saying, "If your partner will have sex with you before you get married, you know one thing about that person—they will have sex with someone they are not married to." He then asked, "How does that make you feel about them going into marriage?" Love is such a gripping emotion that the wisest man of all time, Solomon, said "Do not stir until it satisfies." Love which satisfies literally provides enough to make your mate's soul content. This type of love is the byproduct of time, endurance and character.

Thirdly, it's imperative to ask for the Lord's supernatural strength. When we spend more time yielding to natural satisfaction, it leaves us more susceptible to complications. It's natural to want to go from woman to woman. It's supernatural to nurture just one. It's natural to want every pleasure she can provide. It's supernatural to draw out a plan to work together. Investing more time in the supernatural yields more power to address natural urges and impulses. Thanks to the consequences of some irreversible diseases, we must realize that a booty call can turn into a curtain call at any moment. Increased sexual immorality turns up the chances of our mortality. The person who ignores God's standard is caught in the swift current of fad. The person who embraces God's standard stands at the forefront of a movement.

That which you want *from* a relationship, you ought to bring *to* the relationship since relationships are more about becoming the right person than finding the right person. When you are becoming the right person, the right woman will *be coming* your way. More brothers are looking for a woman than are looking for a wife. If you haven't found the right woman yet, there is more becoming to do. If you have found the right one, there is still more becoming on your agenda. Godly family orientation is one sure mark of manhood. My desire is that you have a relationship so honorable in the sight of the Lord, that others see yours and abandon less honorable ones in favor of ones like yours. Employ God's ideal to minimize life ordeals and the never-ending search for a new deal.

CHAPTER FIVE

AVOID MANHOLES!

─────── **CHECK OUT THIS CHAPTER** ───────

I REFUSE to let you go down a manhole without pouring into your soul some of the words of abundant life that God has poured into mine!

In spite of setbacks, your destiny is still intact.

Every time my dad whipped me, I wanted to return the favor. If I had, someone else would have written this book... and my eulogy!

Manholes don't mug you; they occur in three phases—curiosity, interest and gotcha!

In order to keep a manhole from becoming a black hole, ask God to make you whole in Him.

Superman had kryptonite and every man has a manhole.

─────────────────────────────

"BLUE 41!"

During my freshman year of high school, I played organized football for the first time. At the beginning of the season, we would walk through plays, allowing us to simulate assignments based on our positions. After a dozen or so 'walk-throughs', we would practice at full speed in full equipment so that we could get a better feel for game-time conditions.

"BLUE 41!"

Our football coach had a simple gridiron philosophy—If your head is not in the game, your butt will be on the bench. In route to a 9-1 season, we had some intense practices also known as skull sessions. One skull session in particular will forever stand out! While occupying my usual place on the sideline, the starting offense and defense were scrimmaging, and they had just broken huddle. Evidently the play called by the coach was for the defense and offense to run to the sidelines, find someone not paying attention and hit them-hard!

"HUT, HUT, HUT—HIKE!"

One moment I saw daylight; the next I got clobbered by the starting cornerback whose nickname was "Dr. Death." It was a ferocious hit, executed perfectly—all because I was not paying attention. This sideline scenario is a symbolic snapshot of what could happen in life when we are not paying attention. We can be fully equipped for the game but unaware of what's happening around us or headed toward us.

As you grow, life will move at faster speeds. Each day you should get a better feel for 'lifetime' conditions. This chapter exists primarily for the purpose of slowing your life down a bit to 'walk through' situations so that when you face them, you minimize the number of times you get sacked and the consequent damage that follows. Young men are equipped in many of the same ways an older man is equipped. Are you aware of what's happening in you and around you? If not, you can fall into what I call a "manhole." This is a place in your life so deep that you may not be able to climb out unless someone comes along and gives you a hand.

I clearly remember being rescued from a manhole in the early 1980's. Every summer we would attend our Family Reunion in North Carolina. One year in particular, the gathering was large enough to justify renting a high school gymnasium. In the course of the afternoon, I spotted a cute girl in the crowd. For what seemed like a couple of hours, I tried to get her attention several times—to no avail. When she got up, she headed toward the exit, and I followed her. Having no idea where she was going, I knew that I would have to contrive an 'impromptu' meeting. It turned out that she was headed to the ladie's room. As a last ditch effort, I knocked on the door to the women's bathroom and then ducked into the adjacent men's room. Somehow my dad found out, interrogated me, and he gave me some lasting discipline that same day.

Whippings were a normal part of my upbringing. They were my dad's way of saying, I REFUSE to let you fall into a manhole. Being young and naïve, I did not realize how much pain a manhole could cause but I did realize how much pain *he* could cause. His 'whuppings' used *now* pain, to prevent *later* pain. As backwards as it sounds, this was a pain exchange program where he would give me some immediate pain in order to prevent compounded problems and later pain. Every time my dad whipped me, I wanted to return the favor. If I had, someone else would have written this book and my eulogy. Left unchecked, who knows what manholes I would have fallen into and the pain I would have suffered.

A manhole occurs when we encounter situations or people that are destructive to character and disruptive to growth. Manholes come with hurts, headaches and drama! Whenever the pleasures of God are separated from the purposes of God, only the word of God can re-establish that connection. Because of its potential to threaten your well-being, every manhole ought to be manhandled with the word of God.

A HOLE IN THE SOUL

Personal crisis exposes a deficiency in the soul. Some of what is mentioned next may be out of your purview, but reading about it will groom you for the tests certain to come your way. If you can 'mentally' walk through these dramas, it will help you avert difficulties. Set the stage now for a drama that may occur later, because as author Edwin Lewis Cole said, "It's easier to stay out of temptation than to get out of it."

The enemy does not float generic temptations in your direction. He has studied your preferences and knows precisely where to place the manholes. Since they don't usually look dangerous or deep, his hope is that you will fall in. Once you fall into a manhole, no cute phrases or nursery rhymes will get you out. God knows this, so every manhole comes with an escape hatch. In I Cor. 10:13 (NLT), God reminds us that the temptations in your life are no different than what others experience. And God is faithful. He will not allow the temptation to be more than you can stand. When you are tempted, he will show you a way out so that you can endure." Whether you are talking about a literal or figurative manhole, realize that they are all below you. Don't allow something that is beneath you, to define you.

HOW DEEP IS IT?

Manholes don't mug you—they occur in three stages—curiosity, interest and gotcha. Loiter around any manhole too long and chances increase that you will fall in. Every day is filled with great peril and great potential so, look out for that maaaaanhooooooooleeeeeeeee! No particular manhole will cause you to go to hell, but any of them can attract hellish conditions.

In his best-selling book, *Quiet Strength*, Super Bowl champion coach Tony Dungy mentions to his team the five things that may get you an unflattering write-up in USA Today as: 1. Alcohol or Illegal drugs, 2. Being out after 1:00 a.m., 3. Driving twenty miles over the speed limit, 4. Guns 5. Women you don't know well enough (or that you know too well). Unless you are an incurable hermit, you will have to address most of these issues. Itemized below are several vices which have hampered men for ages. Since there is no such thing as being effective and confused at the same time, establish today where you stand on these matters.

Gangs and Thug Life become a manhole when we are willing to victimize, violate and even kill for the sake of 'swagga'. People in this manhole don't see us all as connected; consequently, it becomes easy to kill without giving a second thought. Problems, frustrations or disappointments are never addressed or solved by taking lives. Alternatives include sports, youth groups, student government, Boy's Club, the military, etc. Each of these allow for the development of healthy relationships with other young men.

Education becomes a manhole when it is not acquired or exercised beneficially. Forsaken education is the prelude to a bogged down life. Learning, is the highway of life's initial opportunities, so when channels of learning are blocked or closed down, future prospects begin to shrivel. During my stints as a substitute teacher and Upward Bound Instructor, I was dismayed by how often the students neglected free instruction. Perhaps the chief hindrance to classroom education is being surrounded by people who aren't there to learn. You will find that many of your peers don't value education, especially in a public school setting. 'Education' comes from the Latin word 'educo' which means to draw out or develop from within. It involves the development of the facilities of your mind as well as managing knowledge. Its purpose is to acquire specific knowledge related to your interest. Measures such as level of education, GPA, and scores on IQ tests are not accurate indicators of knowledge acquisition or potential contribution to society.

We can all garner knowledge from CDs, DVDs and MP3s. Through personal initiative, you can amass more tutelage than offered by any structured institution. Let me ask you something. In the past few months, have you invested more time and money in education or entertainment? Formal education leads you to a job, self-education leads you to establishment. In one sense, the goal of education is to move from comprehension to compensation.

During a telecast of a UNC versus Duke basketball game in the 1990s, the broadcaster said of Duke's ace point guard, Tommy Amaker, "He treats the ball like gold, in that he never turns it over." Your education is like that gold and more. Don't turn it over to class clowns, bullies, laziness, peer pressure, skirt chasing, etc. The objective of education is to accrue knowledge that has been organized and intelligently directed through plans of action.

Lack of Confidence or Lack of Self-Esteem becomes a manhole when feelings of frailty, failure and futility are adopted as a way of life. One avenue to depression occurs when brooding over failure or perceived failure until it envelopes your reality. You are not defined by your skinny legs, big lips, weak jumping ability, Grade Point Average, Body Mass Index, FICO score, time in the 40 yd. dash or bench press. Furthermore, you are not defined by what others think of you. Get the sensation found in Philippians 4:8 (NKJV), which says: "Finally, brethren whatever things are true whatever things are noble, whatever things are just, whatever things are pure, whatever things are lovely, whatever things are of good report, if there is any virtue and if there is anything praiseworthy—meditate on these things." This is the conquering mindset where you can deflect discouragement. Have you added any value to your personal stock today or did you spend it cheering for your favorite athlete who probably doesn't know your name? Identify personal areas of excellence such as singing, dancing, writing, landscaping, cooking, organizing, etc., but know that you are much more significant than your activities because you are fearfully and wonderfully made.

Laziness becomes a manhole when lack of ambition becomes the coffin clasp which confines and asphyxiates manhood. By nature, many of us are lazy, apathetic and vulnerable to base desires. Frankly, I would prefer to have a daily routine where I eat several bowls of ice cream, skip all workouts and sleep for hours on end while watching basketball and action movies from my bed as my children run wild through the house. This would be acceptable if my goal was to have a weight which rivals Jabba the Hut from Star Wars and a home that looks like hell's half acre. Each of us ought to have a definite plan to combat laziness, or it will meet us early in the day and hang out with us all day long. Evaluate your skill set(s) and employ them constantly. In every situation where you decry a lack of opportunity, there is an occasion to exercise your skill set. In order to uncover a dormant skill set, it may be necessary to get some training. When laziness locks in ask and answer two questions. What drives you? What drains you? Move toward the former and away from the latter. Proverbs 12:24(NAS) states that, "The hand of the diligent will rule, but the slack hand will be put to forced labor."

Girls/Women become a manhole when we embrace a debased perspective which permits us to do and say things that devalue them. Without the right perspective of girls/women, this manhole resembles a crater in the soul. As long as any of your five senses are working, this is the inevitable manhole, which author Stephen Arterburn calls "Every Man's Battle." We all have to cross the scorching sands of sexual temptation dozens (perhaps hundreds) of times. Each time you stop and sit on these sands your butt will be burned; therefore, cross these sands quickly! I found this out when

I was 'reading' Playboy magazines. This quickly became a teenage fixation as I wallowed in the pathetic pit of pornography. Clearly, this was not part of God's dream for me. The lens through which I saw women had been so sexually charged that I could not appreciate their substance. Some of my associations were equally demented.

A college buddy of mine often said of his alleged sexual encounters, "She'd better get hers, because I'm sure going to get mine." His remark, reflects today's pervading mindset, one of rollicking lust not responsible love. MSNBC commentator Al Sharpton posed a profound inquiry when he asked, "How can a generation which came from a woman, denigrate that which made them possible?" We have bought into the degradation that others have dumped out for us to lap up like scavengers. When sex is your sole goal, human value and dignity are lost, and you become less of a man and more of an animal. Every time God-given pleasures are separated from their intended purpose, gaping manholes appear.

Money becomes a manhole when it dictates all of our actions and decisions. There are five things to keep in mind as they relates to money. First, prepare for it. Education becomes compensation when knowledge is organized and intelligently directed through plans of action. Second, produce it. Money comes when efforts, services, or ideas are provided in exchange for payment. Every earned dollar in your possession is your employee. Command those employees to bring back good things. It all belongs to God but it's under your management. Third, protect it. Closely scrutinize every institution or advisor who touches your capital. Every day marketers and salespeople devise plans to separate you from your earnings. Devise an informed plan to use your money. Fourth, pass it on. Set up a will so that your possessions and acquired estate will be channeled to designated responsible persons or foundations. Fifth, put it in perspective. The more your life is attached to meaningless things, the less meaning it will have. Abundance is tied to the windows of heaven, not Wall St. Since you are a steward over what belongs to God, always transfer God's tithe, the tenth, and then give a liberal offering.

Personal Disappointment becomes a manhole when you focus on self to the exclusion of helping others or receiving help from them. Often, things go wrong because God is trying to get us right. Some problems are God's employees working on our behalf; don't fire them! Ask Him how to manage these employees. You will make mistakes and in the end, those mistakes will make you. Prolific Author and Pastor, A.W Tozer reflected, "It is doubtful that God can use anyone greatly until He has hurt him deeply." "In times of pressure we discover our actual character. There will always be something for you to overcome. Some of the things bothering you right now will be of no significance six months from now. Pain is one of life's professors; study the circumstances which lead to it.

Develop the strength to transcend hellish situations. One perspective on struggle says that you still have fight left! When you no longer struggle against a problem it means either you have conquered it or been subjugated by it. There is victory in knowing that others have faced and defeated the same difficulty before you now. Take heart in knowing that in spite of setbacks your destiny is still intact.

Relative Truth becomes a manhole when personal values constantly shift to accommodate changing times, and every benchmark from previous generations become negotiable. This is the place where sliding scales have replaced sensible standards. As a consequence, everything imaginable is now allowable. Collectively, these are the clamoring ideas offered as an alternative to defining truth. The notion of 'no absolutes' has been acutely acidic to manhood! Slowly, they have dissolved the enamel of certainty. Relative truth causes an imbalance in the equation of understanding. The story is told of a philosophy professor who began each new term by asking his class, "Do you believe it can be shown that there are absolute values like justice?" The free-thinking students all responded by saying that everything is relative and no single law can be applied universally. Before the end of the semester, the professor devoted one class period to debate the issue. At the end he concluded, "Regardless of what you think, I want you to know that absolute values can be demonstrated. And if you don't accept what I say, I'll flunk you!" One angry student got up and insisted, "That's not fair!" "You've just proven my point," replied the professor. "You've appealed to a higher standard of fairness."

People are relative when it's convenient. Every man ought to ask himself who established the truth he believes? When all ideas are equal, none of them is really valid. Truth predates philosophies and contemporary ideas; it is the highest form of reality. Anything short of it points to an illegitimate ending.

The World Wide Web and New Technology becomes a manhole when they direct time and attention away from the beneficial. I appreciate and respect new technology, but it is so visually stimulating and entertainment-oriented that it steals time from authentic personal development. During an August 2013 interview, Dr. Arch Hart said, "Oxytocin, the intimacy hormone of the brain, gets suppressed when there is an overload of digital technology.

Overloads which occur for months on end, lead to the condition, digital dementia."

There are so many constructive ways to leverage the web. Prov. 17:24 (NLT), the internet-ready scripture says "Sensible people keep their eyes on wisdom but a fool's eyes wander to the ends of the earth." If you've ever come across a racy website, you have seen the 'ends of the earth.' Predetermine what safe sites you will visit and stay there. Set up the computer in a common area to help stay out of trouble. Set blocks of time for internet use so that you eliminate time to drift to an improper site. Don't waste your real life on a virtual life.

FILLING THE HOLE

No doubt that the easel of your life will be splattered with mistakes too. We all have defects; until we get help, they will constrict us. Fortunately for us, "Rescue is the constant pattern of God's activity," according to Frances Fariginpere. That's likely because mess-up is the constant pattern of man's activity. In the middle of every difficulty are the letters i-c-u, God says, "I c u" as an overcomer. Although difficulties are inevitable, God gave us the ability to scale them. That's why He calls you an overcomer. Contrary to instinct, God is made strong in our weaknesses. Manholes represent the place of loss, but lasting recovery starts with Divinity.

In order to keep a manhole from becoming a black hole, ask God to make you whole in Him . If you have been in a manhole so long that it has grown on you, amputate it with a word from the Bible. This is the power given to you, and it's vital to face the challenges coming against you. This is not an accidental reading at an incidental time. Because you are reading these words, it is obvious that you are woven into the fabric of my destiny—by the provision of God, I REFUSE to let you go into a manhole without pouring into your soul, some of the words of truth and abundant life that God has poured into mine!!

CHAPTER SIX

GROWTH
MANAGEMENT

My personal preferences didn't always matter to
a father who was more concerned about building
character in his sons than catering to their whims.

With one trifling exception, the entire
world is made up of other people.

Components are useless until they are
connected—you are a component in God's
kingdom. Where are you connected?

God arranges life so that we can all benefit
from each other, thereby fulfilling his dream
of a people that are concerned about
each other and connected to Him.

THE ONLY PLACE YOU CAN COAST IS DOWNHILL

While in the Cub Scouts, I learned some indispensable
life-skills such as respect, courtesy, reverence, honesty,

patriotism, camping, and cooking. As those lessons were being taught, my mind would usually drift ahead to the time when we were dismissed to go outside and run around. Aside from eating the pancakes we cooked while camping, I did not really like being in the scouts. At home, my personal preferences didn't always matter to a father who was more concerned about building character in his sons than catering to their whims. Bona fide parenting will frequently impinge upon a child's 'rights' in an effort to steer him to development. Growth management of boys is obligatory because *man* is what *age* is *meant* to bestow upon boys. It's highly unfortunate that boys don't always want to grow up and act like men. Welcome to life in Quadrant II, the tense turning point between taking it easy and taking things seriously.

BOYS ARE RESISTANT TO TRAINING

I remember thinking that the only reason my parents had me was to do *their* housework! Many of my days were spent on an endless list of chores: sweeping floors, vacuuming floors, cleaning toilets, washing dishes, washing cars, washing windows, painting rooms, installing electrical fixtures, installing storm windows, chopping wood, hanging pictures, pulling weeds, cutting grass, raking leaves, bathing the dog, etc. I did not have an ounce of doubt that all of this was a ploy by my parents to curb my fun. Without my knowledge or consent, my parents were intentionally setting me up for the responsibilities of manhood.

From a boy's perspective, all I felt was that I was being exploited, not benefitting from child labor laws. How could two people be so cruel?!! Didn't they know that there were neighborhood football games to play, comic books to trade, girls to call, woods to explore, bikes to ride, and an Atari 2600 to play?! I thought my schedule was too full for housework. Who needs housework? After all, the Yellow Pages were full of people who were eager to do the housework I dreaded!

It was not until after I grew up and moved out, that I understood, every chopping motion, sweeping motion and washing motion represented one more thread in the tapestry of my manhood. Each chore was part of preparation that could only be imparted by parents who were deliberate about training their children in the way they should *grow*. There are four specific growth pursuits necessary for total life cultivation: mental, spiritual, social, and physical.

Like a police officer in hot pursuit of a dangerous criminal, you ought to track down these growth pursuits at top speed, over any obstacle, under any circumstances, and at any time until you corner them, capture them and contain them. You can then announce to your partners," I have them in custody." In fact, your partners will know that you have captured them long before you make the announcement. Indispensable is the man in possession of this coveted quartet.

PREPARTION IS SEPARTION

Boys avoid the prospect of doing difficult things. Men embrace opportunities to stretch, grow and advance. Preparation is separation—from the boys at the bottom of the pack to the men at the top of the stack! If we are looking for the premium example of preparation, our search culminates with Jesus Christ. In the second chapter of the book of Luke, verse 52, the author's observation of Jesus gives us a powerful, practical and complete picture of preparation. Here, Luke articulates the four-dimensional development of Jesus. Jesus grew in wisdom, stature and in favor with God and with men. That is to say, He grew mentally, spiritually, socially, and physically. Each of these growth aspects is a mile marker in establishing Godly masculinity.

IF YOU WANNA BE STEADY, YOU GOTTA STUDY

And Jesus grew in wisdom... **Mental growth occurs when receiving and applying practical guidance for skillful living. The man who is growing mentally constantly asks and answers the question, what am I becoming?**

If your purpose for studying is to get good grades through grit, effort or smarts—you will eventually get them; at the same time you might miss the essence of the drills. If your purpose for drills and studying is to get understanding, then you will obtain good grades, knowledge and understanding in such a way that you are distinguished from your peers. So imperative is understanding, that Proverbs 4:7 (NKJV) states, "in all of your getting, get understanding." Pastor A.R. Bernard declared, "That which we do not understand will be eventually stolen from us." Comprehension bolsters all of your study material. Opportunities for study and mental growth are in abundance through museums, books, blogs, community colleges, community centers, elderly people, forums, etc.

When I was in high-school, a memorable mental growth moment occurred during a heated head-to-head discussion with my father. We were emphatically discussing the benefits and burdens of taking 12th grade Advanced Placement English Literature. He wanted me to take this class while

I sought the easier way. My argument was, "Dad, isn't it better to make an 'A' in a 'B' level course than to make a 'B' in an "A" level course? It was a battle of wills between my desire to take an easier route versus dad's desire for me to learn the value of accepting a challenge. While I was angling for the best grade, dad wanted me to have the strongest challenge. I wanted to *pass* the class and he wanted me to *surpass* the class. Dad won, and in the end, so did I. I took that AP English course and earned the credits necessary to place out of college-level English Literature. These are the defining moments, the types of challenges that separate the men from the boys.

It is daunting and discouraging to see that some public schools have become drop-out factories where 60% or fewer of the incoming freshmen graduate. Even if you are not inclined to be a so-called, top student, here are a few practical pointers which will give you the mental edge no matter where you go to school—prepare to surpass! The 'preparing man' can physically occupy his current level of living while mentally operating on a higher level of living.

CASES IN POINT:

Inquire and Invest : Everyone watches television, but the 'preparing man' goes out to the station to interview the director or producer. Many people fly on airplanes; the 'preparing man' reads the book to find out what inspired its invention. Throngs of people shop at the local Megamart; the 'preparing man' probes the mind of entrepreneurs to discover how the economic phenomenon was developed and how he too can benefit.

Inquire and Invest: Every student walks past the principal's office (hoping not to ever have to go there); the 'preparing man' sets an appointment with the principal to find out how the school is run.

Extras for Excellence: When my high school Trigonometry teacher assigned the even numbered math problems as homework, I completed the even and odd numbered math problems throughout the school year. This approach helped me to secure one of the highest math scores on the Henrico County Standardized Math Test that year.

When I needed pointers for delivering a talk for an oratorical contest, I enlisted the help of my pastor who, not only gave me tips, but set aside time during the Sunday morning service of several hundred worshipers for me to deliver that talk. That type of exposure helped me win both regional and national oratorical contests. In order to develop some academic tenacity, I attended several summer camps at state colleges, taking everything from computer programming, to Calculus and volleyball. These occurrences fostered collegiate confidence. It's in the doing of extra that your capacity gets expanded and excellence becomes your brand.

Dare to Go Big: My second time experiencing this 'go big' principle occurred in college. It was then that my engineering organization sponsored a technical paper contest with a free trip to a conference in Los Angeles, CA as the grand prize. Having never before written a technical paper, I was hesitant to enter. Using the content of a research paper I had written the previous semester, I took the plunge. There were a couple of friends who helped me organize it and make it look professional. I submitted that work and to my amazement, it was deemed the winning essay. I was invited to present it at a national conference in Los Angeles. Later that year it was published in a national magazine. As I inquired about the other contestants, I discovered that only a handful of people entered. What a boost that was! I had never flown before or won a national contest. Entering and winning that contest gave me to confidence to enter and win similar contests in subsequent years.

Treat Life Like a Research Paper: First, attend a trial to see how the legal system works. Before joining a gang, vicariously experience the finality of a jail sentence. Secondly, see if you can shadow a professional in order to learn about a career before committing to it. When reading and exploring, learn for the sake of application not just higher education. No matter what's going on, ask lots of 'why' questions. Tag along with adults who vote and ask them to produce the strongest reasons as to why they vote the way they do. My children have 'voted' since they were two-years old by pushing the button I told them to push.

These are all activities of the preparing man. The things he does transcends the classroom and industry. Paul L. Dunbar, the 19th century African-American poet said, "The mind is the standard of the man." How do you stock your standard? Many read only for entertainment; the 'preparing man' has a purposeful reading program implemented for his educational and entrepreneurial benefit. When you are on top of your game, you can develop the sagacity to change the game. A 'preparing man' can live in the projects while he pries his mind and attitude free from that setting. Do the people who are part of your association mentally stretch you?

BODY OF WORK

And Jesus grew in stature (Luke 2:52) NIV...**Physical growth occurs when men utilize wholesome provision to cultivate well-being. The man who is growing physically** asks the question: **How can I leverage fitness as a way of life?** Being in shape starts inside and works its way out. A robust attitude precedes a vigorous health profile. My long distance track coach, who was also a Judo Black Belt, made us 'train in tough conditions so that the track meet would be a breeze.' We would suit up to practice in eighty-degree weather wearing fully hooded sweat suits. A different coach, on that same championship team, reminded us, "It's a long road to get in shape but an easy road out of shape."

In order to take shape, cater to the internal mechanisms of the body. Take these steps to grow healthy. Stimulate your body with filtered water, wholesome food, necessary supplements, specific exercise, and periods of tranquility.

Around 960 b.c., King Solomon built a temple for the Lord so exquisite, that it was held together with solid gold nails. Holy Scripture tells us that our bodies are temples of the Lord, infinitely more valuable than any temple built by man's hands. This is an indication of the body's value. Cherish it more than your favorite automobile; it is infinitely more precious. When it comes to proactively advancing your health, here are five solid gold nails to promote and to preserve robust health.

1. Wake up with Water—I once read about an eighty-year-old who gave his secret for long

life. He started his day with an 8oz glass of water to wake up the digestive system and hydrate his cells. Cells are the basic building block of your body and water is the optimum greeting for the encounter of each new day. With diabetes, stress, high cholesterol and high blood pressure causing mayhem in personal health care, make sure that water factors heavily in the fight against these complications. Many start the day by shocking their digestive system with sugary food. Filtered water gently activates a dormant digestive system so that it can receive fresh fruits for breakfast.

2. Consume food as fuel, not just filler: Make a daily determination to eat several healthy meals, then pack them and take them with you! There ought to be daily staples in your diet that announce to your cells, tissues and organs, "You are all important to me, so I give you premium care." Intentionally consume foods that cause your body chemistry to be alkaline, less acidic. Acidic bodies harbor conditions that are receptive to

diseases, while alkaline bodies host good health. Alkaline foods include spinach and broccoli, kale, peas, blueberries and sour cherries. As my wife often says, "You don't have to like them, just eat them!" In fact, name the five healthy items you ate yesterday. _____ , _____ , _____ , _____ , _____ . What are the five healthy items you intend to eat today? _____ , _____ , _____ , _____ , _____ .

3. Several years ago, I stopped eating pork. Although I had enjoyed it in various forms, I accepted the challenge which says, "Control your diet or your diet will control you!" I dare you to eliminate one of your favorites from your diet. If there ever comes a time that you need to, you know that you can.

4. Supplement for sustenance and to stave off sickness—Become mighty through micro nutrition. Do you have a family history of diabetes? Employ fiber, fiber rich foods, and chromium to help regulate blood sugar

levels. Do you know of uncles, cousins or grandparents with Prostate cancer? Employ saw palmetto, tomatoes and lutein to foster a healthy prostate gland. Is your clan prone to high blood pressure? Employ garlic, green tea, and omega three in the service of managing blood pressure. Find out which recurring family health issues you could possibly face. Research it and proactively prepare your body to handle it.

5. Stretch and strengthen through specific exercise. We all have target areas of our bodies that could benefit from being more fit. Consult a respected trainer or source for ideal cardio care. Find or design a program that caters to your fitness needs. It need not be a cost prohibitive program because push-ups, jumping jacks and planking exercises are all free!

6. Take time for tranquility: While hordes of people have been diagnosed with ADHD and ADD, many suffer from PDD, that is Peace Deficit Disorder. Fresh air, quiet time,

and deep breaths are all necessary to disarm this disorder. Turning off all noise and electronic devices is especially important in a bustling metropolis. Embrace blocks of peace, so that you don't waste life in turmoil. Turn off all outside influences. One insurance company uses its commercials to proclaim that "mayhem is everywhere." Eject it from your day by setting aside time to relax, reflect and breathe deeply. Pregnant women take cleansing breaths as they prepare to bring forth a new life. That is a metaphor for bringing forth a new life of tranquility. Replenish like never before.

Question about physical condition: When was your last thorough health examination given by a doctor? Do you consult a nutritionist or a book on nutrition? What changes did it cause you to make?

CONNECT AND CONTRIBUTE

And Jesus grew in favor with men (Luke 2:52) NIV…**Social growth occurs when demonstrating the loving heart of God by initiating, establishing and building relationships.**

The boy asks, "What can someone else do for me?" The man who is growing socially asks the question, "Am I connecting and contributing to the lives of others?"

Just as a home entertainment center has components that all work together to create a far-reaching effect, so too are we. Components are useless until they are connected— you are a component in God's kingdom, connected by serving others. With one trifling exception, the entire world is made up of other people and creations. Communities, clubs and churches serve as outlets to connect, share and grow. Social growth is key because working together precedes winning together.

The challenge is that the enemy of your soul wants to frustrate all of your relationships. The first relationship he wants to rupture is the parental or guardian relationship, then that of the siblings and extended family, followed by that of the primary woman in your life. The deeper the division, the more satisfied he is. Like a banana that has been separated from its bunch, one of two things will occur when you are isolated from relationships. Either there will be consumption or corruption. Disconnection is the preview for becoming consumed with guilt, laziness, selfishness, lust, etc. The enemy of your soul has a goal of corrupting your legitimacy by bringing you to a point of separation, frustration, isolation and annihilation.

It behooves us to be socially conscious and socially connected, now! Here's how:

Develop an awareness and appreciation for the contributions of pioneers and ancestors. Ken Burns, author of The War, states that, "Responsibility, the notion of shared sacrifice, is something we've forgotten to do and do so at our peril." Determine what names like Maggie Walker, Ida B. Wells, Ghandi, Frederick Douglas, etc. mean to you? Get fresh inspiration from 'old' people. Visit or serve at a VA hospital, children's hospital, nursing home or place of mental illness.

Exercise your gifts. No matter the economic or social conditions, there will *always* be a strong demand for outstanding men and women. The smart man is able to identify what God is doing, the wise man joins Him. Are you preparing to become the world-class man that society craves?

Question about social condition: What group activity are you involved in that stretches you?

THE NEW YOU TRUTH EXCHANGE

And Jesus grew in favor with God (Luke 2:52) NIV...
**Spiritual growth occurs when connecting to the Lord God
in personal relationship and serving others. The boy asks,
"What is God going to do for me?" The man asks, "How
am I connecting and how am I serving the Lord God?"**

It's important to cultivate your spiritual development
because you are a spirit housed in a body. Mental growth
and spiritual growth are tightly woven together. The mind,
body, and spirit are such close neighbors that when one
gets sick the other two may soon catch what the first has.
Spiritual wellness is a result of taking daily doses of truth.
If we commit to doing this daily, however, we face a challenge. We are all subject to a barrage of experiences wherein
the full weight of emphasis is on 'having fun'. 'Give me the
thrilling instead of the fulfilling' is the motto of our times.

Like spending a day at the amusement park, a soul that
does not or cannot latch on to something that is fulfilling
will float from thrill to thrill until it is exhausted. That
soul is reduced to the same shallow existence of the masses,
thirsty for the next thrill. Having dined all day on spiritual
cotton candy and sno-cones, you go home at sundown mal-
nourished and exhausted, yet come to the conclusion, "I
gotta do that again!" The experience comes to a close with

the person having been entertained but the soul not edified. At that point the person arrives at a place of spiritual stagnation followed by boredom then trouble. It is the robust combination of spiritual tenacity and serving tendency which nurtures spiritual growth.

This chapter boils down to the choice of pleasure chasing versus personal development. Physically speaking, idleness and ice cream are chosen more often than healthy alternatives. In the mental realm, more people will talk about the latest sitcom than the book they are reading. It's certainly easier to ignore people than to start a conversation and make a connection. Each day we see more examples of spiritual depravity than nobility. Integrating mental, social, physical and spiritual qualities will cause you to develop into a viable and reliable person. Every man ought to have the described Luke 2:52 program encoded in his spirit.

Civil rights leader, Whitney Young declared, "It is better to be prepared for an opportunity and not have one than to have an opportunity and not be prepared for it." All who are prepared will find opportunity. If by chance you don't find one, step up and create one. When we comprehend, we can combat the strategies designed to keep us economically defeated, spiritually distant, mentally disinterested, and socially disconnected. God arranges life so that we can all benefit from each other, thereby fulfilling His dream of a people who are concerned about each other and connected to Him. Grambling University football coaching legend, Eddie Robinson lived by the credo, "You have to coach 'em as though he were the boy who was going to marry your daughter." There are many who want to master the 'art' of womanizing; this chapter challenges those who want to be fabulous suitors for someone's daughter. Continuous growth is yet another feature of those on the road to manhood.

CHAPTER SEVEN

MENTORED
BY TORMENT

Talk about a smackdown, my scrawny grade
point average was body-slammed by the
bodacious tag-team combination of Calculus
II, Physics, Statics and PASCAL Programming.

Take the loyalty of a baseball fan that will stick
around for extra innings—baptize it—and stick
around for the birth and growth of your children.

Take the determination to find a woman at
the club who will let you 'hit it'—baptize it—
and find a job that will let you work it!

I give you God's word, because His word
is the black box that remains intact after a
crash into the side of life's mountains.

A man who goes without hope for
extended periods of time soon
wants others to feel his plight.

Everything dismal demands baptismal.

Properly angled, every experience can be parlayed into progress.

'Two semesters of dejection' is what I call the academic year subsequent to the letter stating that I would be placed on academic probation. This was the one hardship I never expected to encounter. After reading this letter, my thoughts flashed back to the time just before the start of my freshman year. It was then I had assured myself, that 'I would put Old Dominion University on my back and take it to the promised land!' With all the confidence that comes with ignorance, I was certain that I would make top grades, become a model student, and earn a place in the hallowed halls of academia. I was sure that I would make the Dean's List. It turns out that I only qualified to make the Dean's prayer list!

AP status was not new, per se. In high school I took Advanced Placement courses and was hailed as an AP student. In college however, that same label was, for me, a 'Scarlet Letter' and a telltale sign of scholastic instability. How did this happen? Talk about a smack down! My scrawny grade point average had been body-slammed by the bodacious tag-team combination of Calculus II, Physics, Statics and PASCAL Programming. As a footnote,

PASCAL is now an obsolete programming language. That is to say, some of the things that worry you now are slated for obsolescence. Futility in its highest form occurs when we worry about something that will soon fade away. What a turn of events—I had left high school with high commendations; now my confidence was floating in the commode. I started out with great promise, so how did I end up in this predicament? Was there a great reason for this experience?

Compared with some life issues, academic probation is not that big of a deal. There are schools that will admit you no matter how wretched your academic record. Just about anyone can get admitted into school and develop the character to graduate. How we rebound from personal defeats usually depends on perspective coupled with readiness to make course corrections.

In this chapter we will consider several undesirable, even criminal scenarios; some of which you may have experienced in the past or be experiencing right now. We will then reframe them and propose a mature pursuit as an alternative. We will also determine how to take torment and get mentorship from it. The strengths of a Quadrant 3 man are displayed here. Their handling of problems incites those same qualities in those around him.

PROBLEM, USHER ME TO THE FRONT ROW!

Everyone reading this script has challenges to address, no matter how diligently you attempt to avoid them. God has customized a set of problems specifically for your growth. The solution-oriented man realizes that a problem is a stimulant, a prelude to a scene change. For instance, is the problem that she gets on your nerves? Or is this the prelude to identifying different things you can do together? Is the problem that you have an attention deficit disorder? Or is this the catalyst to finding a dynamic learning approach that can accommodate your edgy learning style? Don't always heed the prescribed notion of education and pedigree. Is the problem that you can't find a job or is this your prelude to creating a job?

In America, there is a market for just about everything. If you are skilled in the game of basketball, then you can play for a high school, a church league, a summer league, the Harlem Globetrotters, the NBA, an overseas team, street ball or the _____ phenomenon (which *you* have yet to invent). If the solution is unknown to you, today is the perfect day for producing it. Remember that flight pioneer Orville Wright did not have a pilot's license. Renowned poetess Phyllis Wheatley was not listed amongst Who's Who when she started writing poetry. Understanding the problem provides the raw tools for dismantling it.

When problems are stacked or extended for a period of time, they can foster a feeling of torment. How is it possible to turn a tormenting time into a mentoring tool? It's called perspective. If there is no platform to address your difficulty, you are a prime candidate to construct that platform. If you are talented, you will be tormented.

THROW THE TALENT SWITCH

You have talents unrecognized by your own eyes. Have you decided to use that talent for evil or good? There comes a time in the life of every boy/man when he has to decide how to use his talents. Growing up, my dad and I would have foot races in the narrow space between our home and our neighbor's house. It seemed as though I could never keep pace with him, so I sought a different opponent. While the cars would drive up and down the street in front of our home, I would 'race' them by running on the sidewalk. As I dashed in the 'hood', I could have decided to use that sprinting talent for evil—such as running from the police. Those 'races' gave birth to a competitive thirst as well as a love for running track. Eventually they became the basis for success in track meets where I participated in 800 meter, High Jump and Long Jump events. Every talent can be used for evil or edification.

In the early 1980's, I got my first bike. Along with that bike came a simple parental instruction: stay within earshot of the house. It didn't take long to push that boundary. Pretty soon, I was on the other side of the neighborhood getting comic books and candy at the convenience store. That one dose of disobedience led to a period of time when I would frequently visit that same store and get comic books and candy without paying for them. Used for good, the talent of bike riding can build stamina. Used for evil, that same talent can be used to take comic books and candy without paying for them.

Talents which are pointed north, toward making a contribution, produce hope. Talents which are pointed south, toward helping only yourself, generate despair. A man who goes without hope, soon wants others to feel his plight. If he is without hope for extended periods of time, he will begin to impose that hopelessness on others. This marks the beginning of criminal tendencies. Repossess that hopeless attitude, tow it to the junkyard, and pick up a late model attitude showcased in Romans 15:13 (NIV) where the God of hope fills you with all joy and peace as you trust in Him, so that you may overflow with hope by the power of the Holy Spirit. I give you God's word, because His word is the only thing left after a crash into the side of life's mountain. Jesus is known for lots of things. Let's use the next few paragraphs to examine Him as the savior of our behavior, as well as our souls.

TAKE IT AND BAPTIZE IT!

Ephesians 4:28 (NLT) says, "If you are a thief, stop stealing. Begin using your hands for honest work, and then give generously to others in need." Even when we are in destructive patterns, Christ is primed to do an astounding work in our lives. When allowed, He will strip us of our pursuits but not our passions. For every problem, you can baptize it. 'Baptize it' in this case means to seize and extract value from a destructive or non-productive situation. After you seize it reconfigure it until values comes forth. When talents are connected to opportunity, hope flourishes. Here we will talk about the reconfiguring. In the MANgoes chapter, we will connect it to opportunity.

Take the ability to be a look out man (for the police)-baptize it—and forecast the weather or the economy. Take the knack to slip in and out of the house in the middle of the night—baptize it—and become a private investigator. Take the desire to sneak all over town and be on the down low with multiple men—baptize it and become an event coordinator. Take the 'smarts' needed to pimp women-baptize it and run franchises! Take the skill set needed to set up drug deals—baptize it and become a City Manager! Take the capacity to coordinate gang activity—baptize it and run a security detail! Take the charisma needed to get the whole club bouncing—baptize it and raise social, political and spiritual awareness. Take the passion to memorize player profiles, game summaries and fantasy league stats—baptize it and dominate algebra! Take the speed needed to outrun the police—baptize it and train for competitive athletics. Take the cleverness required to cover your tracks—baptize it and establish a good track record. Take your 'playa playa' reputation—baptize it and help a sistah to see her beauty beyond her booty. Take the brashness needed to carry out a home invasion robbery—baptize it and deliver the truth door to door. Take the conniving conduct of a swindler— baptize it into the savvy needed to manage a portfolio. Take bartending talents—baptize them and conquer chemistry. Take the calculating mind of a pool shark-baptize it and excel in trigonometry and geometry. Take the stealth ways of a pickpocket—baptize them and become a talent scout. Take the impromptu flow of a 'freestyle' rapper-baptize it and translate foreign languages. Take the propensity to fix the blame—baptize it and fix the problem. Take pent-up aggression—baptize it and become the foreman of a demolition team. Take the smooth talk necessary to find women who will clothe, house and feed you—baptize it and raise funds for national organizations. Take the tendency to steal and strip cars-baptize it and build circuit boards and motherboards. Take the loyalty of a baseball fan who will stick around for extra innings—baptize it and stick around for the birth and growth of your babies. Take the patience, persistence and perception necessary to hack corporate websites—baptize it and discover cures for Crohn's Disease, Alzheimers, HPV and Autism.

Take the determination to scope a neighborhood until you find someone to rob—baptize it and input data into GPS programs. Take the observation skill necessary to stalk someone—baptize it and become an air traffic controller.

Take the determination to find a woman at the club who will let you 'hit it'—baptize it and find a job that will let you work it!

In life, everything dismal demands baptismal. To find mentorship in the midst of torment, employ your defects in the service of your assets. The more we turn to the Lord, the more beneficial creations, inventions, and innovations

He gives us. The more we turn from the Lord, the more inadequate we become.

Every conceivable evil is one calculated U-turn away from becoming something meaningful. Inside of every predicament lies a promise for productivity. We all have tremendous capacity to unleash evil or inspire excellence. According to author Dennis Kimbro, "Within you lies a power which, when properly grasped and directed, can lift an entire race out of the rut of mediocrity, poverty and failure and onto the shores of fortune." Because such breathtaking potential resides within you, you are often in the news, frequently being watched and sometimes being followed. Usually "Breaking News" and "Developing Story" publicize more stories about a man or men who are breaking than those who are developing.

TALES FROM THE BAPTISMAL POOL

For the redeemed soul, 'Baptize it' occurs daily. Malcolm X took a jail sentence and baptized it until it became a social movement. Wilma Rudolph took diseased legs and baptized them until they galloped to Olympic Gold. Gideon of the Midianite tribe, baptized his anemic self-image in the might of the Holy Spirit, then led the Midianite military to victory. Ghandi absorbed British oppression and baptized it until it became a national peace mission.

Although we are unbelievably creative at messing up good things, we can submit any disaster to the Master and he will give mentorship from torment. Even if you have brought the torment upon yourself—as we all do—torment is the welcome mat to maturity. Through methodical maturity, men can rise above setbacks, an indisputable trait of manhood. Mature men endeavor to shift gears from the superficial to the supernatural. This allows you to form a pattern of strength upon which others can feed. Genesis 50:20 is the ultimate 'turn around' scripture, it says "what man meant for evil, God meant for good." You can rise from any demise if you offer your dilemma to Him and allow Him to turn it into something remarkable.

CHAPTER EIGHT

A THINKING MAN'S GAME (1ST HALF)

─────── CHECK OUT THIS CHAPTER───────

Your mind is your very first and finest 'real estate' investment. How's your mental real estate market?

Brain power is the main power missing from the daily regimen of a man.

Clear thinking is based on truth.

It's important to think because thinking is fundamental to progress.

It's important to think critically because time moves quickly and works on behalf of the critical thinker who takes action.

It's important to think clearly because thoughts are linked to actions and actions are connected to consequences.

Brace yourself like a man, (Job 38:3) NIV

Soon after arriving at the university to begin my freshman year, I sought the mentorship of the upperclassmen who were engineering majors. Their insight and advice were important to me, because I aspired to make it to their level of academic standing. From every indication, engineering majors faced a difficult curriculum. In one instance, the Instructor for an Introduction to Engineering class said to an auditorium packed with freshmen, "Look to your left, look to your right and look at yourself. Only one of those three people will be here at graduation." In a separate freshman orientation session, we were told that there was an 85% attrition rate among minorities in the engineering program.

Both of those challenging statements simmered in my, soul and they could have caused me fear or discouragement, leading me to succumb to statistics. Instead, I decided to let them stoke my motivational coals and power me through the five grueling years of Electrical Engineering and Technology studies that lay ahead. Instead of adopting victimology, I felt led to express my silent condolences to the others in my class, knowing that I would march to a degree.

Although I didn't know the entire process, or the associated challenges, I had an inner confirmation that I would earn a degree. I drew strength from the assurance of my father that

I was there for higher education, not higher embarrassment. From his numerous overcoming examples, I decided to "brace myself like a man" and face the full brunt of the program. I resolved to turn that notion into full-time action!

Carter G. Woodson, that timeless scholar and journalist declared, "When you control a man's thinking, you do not have to worry about his actions. You do not have to tell him not to stand here or go yonder. He will find his 'proper place' and stay in it. You do not need to send him to the back door. He will go without being told. In fact, if there is no door, he will cut one for his special benefit." Armed with that type of insight, you too can leverage any itch to increase. Woodson knew that a man's mind is one of his most important assets. What we think and believe determines the quality of that invisible ground inside our heads. **Your mind is your very first and finest real estate investment. How's your mental real-estate market?**

Whether you are in elementary school or mastering life at the management level in your career, it's time to prepare for higher education. To be a truly educated man is to develop and maintain a voracious appetite for useful and constructive knowledge. Every book you read and every course you take is an investment in that essential real estate known as your mind. You can maintain and improve it daily, or treat it as a dumping ground. Each guy ought to evaluate himself by asking: With what am I filling my mind? Where are my thoughts leading me? A quick review of your tasks and activities from the past week gives an indication of the direction in which you are headed.

I determined that I would move onward to manhood with my chosen degree and profession. In order to do so, I used, developed and disciplined my mind.

Your mind is a terrible thing to waste, and waste is a terrible thing to a mind. You are today where yesterday's thoughts have brought you. Tomorrow you will be where today's thoughts take you. What occupies your mind determines the place in life you will occupy. Be judicious about what goes into your mind.

IF IT IS RIDICULOUS, THEN IT WILL BE REPORTED

No matter when you are reading this, you will easily be able to name three headline events from the past week that seem highly absurd. Not long ago, the media reported that the son of an NFL Hall of Famer was arrested for the same sex crimes as his father. A couple of weeks after that, I read of a father/son duo who were arrested on charges of pimping. Did these four guys really expect to get away with that kind of misconduct?

A barrage of influences including smart phones, Ipads, videos, 24-hour-whatever channels, trashy magazines, and mindless chatter contribute to John Q. Public's brain stupor. Too many of us never learn how to think for ourselves because we rarely exercise our thinking capacity. We absorb hours of useless information and even trash the real estate of our minds.

What we need is foundational thinking as a way to claim and regain the fertile ground inside our skulls and build ourselves as intelligent men who have significance and relevance in this era. By foundational thinking I mean developing the valuable and necessary ability to take information and process it through a grid of wisdom until we come to the right conclusion for any situation we encounter.

Brain power is the main power missing from the daily regimen of men today. People are parched from a severe drought of clear thinking. Because of that, many have lost the ability to make critical decisions. This point in time has been called the Information Age; however, many are missing the information necessary for transformation. Thoughts are the ingredients that nourish or starve life. Junky thoughts are the hollow ingredients which lead to a life starved for attentiveness and hungry for fulfillment. Truly nourishing thoughts energize by building strong bones of belief. A polluted thought life sabotages peace and usually precedes a bogged down life.

When thoughts flash in your mind, you can either flush them or flesh them out. You will move on without them or be mired down by them. In the Thinking MAN's Game, there are six probing questions to ask and answer. Are you thinking? Are you thinking clearly? Are you thinking critically? Are you thinking creatively? Are you thinking correctly? Are you thinking constantly? In this chapter we will explore the first three questions. Move on from here and you begin to exit Quadrant 3.

ARE YOU THINKING?

This question represents the jump ball of the Thinking Man's Game. Thinking occurs when the mind is used to form a series of beliefs that direct your actions. It's important to think because thinking is fundamental to progress. You will be stimulated and inspired by what you see most often. Your mind has to be able to process what it sees and its worth, relative to your mission, yet how often do males make decisions based on what they've heard in popular song lyrics and celebrity tweets? The choices we make based on other men's common opinions, renders us no better than hearing casual conversations.

In reality, we are all followers when it comes to all that we know and need to learn about life, living, relationships and correct beliefs. The secret lies in knowing whose thoughts to follow. If you are going to follow someone, follow the right one! The first and second halves of the Thinking Man's Game offers pointers on how to identify those right people. There is only one true foundation for your mind that delivers a complete source of insight and wisdom. God, in the form of Jesus Christ, offers that comprehensive example. Malachi 3:16b (NIV) declares, "In his presence, a scroll of remembrance was written to record the names of those who feared the Lord and honored his name." As often as possible, think about the honor of His name. Albert Einstien, one of history's masterminds said, "I want to think the thoughts of God; the rest are details."

Many rely on human intellect as their supreme source. Intellect is greatly overmatched when it has a 'jump ball' with the truth. "The most potent weapon in the hands of the oppressor is the mind of the oppressed", said Steven Biko, South African Revolutionary. What that means is it's dangerous to let others—especially others who want you to serve their purposes—do the thinking for you. There are people in this world who count on you to mindlessly do exactly what they say, using your time, money, and energy to do precisely what they want you to do.

Scenario: You have not established good health or hygiene habits. It's now imperative that you visit the doctor for some urgent care. How will you handle this important visit? Realize that, the same money you have for a visit to the emergency room is the same money that can be used to invest in a doctor's appointment and follow-up. Doctors can't treat macho, but you can. What is the next move for a man who is thinking?

ARE YOU THINKING CLEARLY?

This question represents the timeout during the Thinking Man's Game. It is important to think clearly because your thoughts are connected to your actions and actions are connected to consequences. I Peter1:13 (NIV) encourages us with these words, "Therefore, prepare your minds for action, be self-controlled; set your hope fully on the grace to be given you when Jesus Christ is revealed."

Looking forward and making decisions from a clear thinking standard of truth gives you a tremendous advantage over your peers. Trendy or unclear thinking tends to be widely accepted, yet it is bound to wobbly opinions. So much of what used to be called common sense has disappeared that nonsense has become normal.

Clear thinking is based on truth; it always has been and it always will be. As truth is deposited often enough and deeply enough, it becomes conviction. When the truth is engraved in your heart and mind, you cannot be enslaved by peer pressure. Conviction is another hallmark of becoming a mature man;

it's the Twitter hashtag of a Quadrant 3 man. Convictions stabilize and without them, men are destined to be swept away by the currents of faddish thinking. Clarity becomes clutter when non-negotiables are compromised.

Does your thinking seem cluttered? If so, look around and listen up. Is your environment cluttered with noise and items? Thoughts birthed in a chaotic and polluted mind cannot be fully developed. Too much external stimuli will suppress your inner man, so designate a time to turn it off. Good ideas come from taking walks and putting external stimuli on hold. Stop and manage life instead of being enmeshed in it.

Scenario: With two Ds and one F on my tests, I'm in an academic bind. The upcoming fourth test is an opportunity to redeem myself. Through my 'connections' I have downloaded a copy of the test questions onto my IPad. By discreetly using an earphone and software that reads text, I could cheat and no one would ever know. Here's my dilemma: If I fail this class, my GPA falls below the minimum required to stay on the team. Flunking means I will not get to play in the state finals in front of the college scouts who have expressed an interest in me. Just this one time I need to make the grade!

Write out the next move for a man who is thinking clearly. How important is this moment to your college aspirations? How important is this moment to your integrity? What are the consequences of thinking incorrectly? Are there consequences for cheating if no one finds out? Is it considered cheating if no one finds out? Realize that today is the past you will have to face tomorrow.

You are thinking clearly when you can observe that your life is aligned for blessings not consequences.

ARE YOU THINKING CRITICALLY?

This question sets the tempo for the Thinking Man's Game. It is important to think critically because time moves quickly and works on behalf of the critical thinker. Critical thinking is based on sound strategy and leaves room for error and improvement. Without it, one relies on happenstance and makes decisions that lack systematic consideration. Critical decision makers find their basis in existing strengths, whereas the reckless blindly hope for achievement in the absence of clear-cut strength. Prov. 13:16 (NLT) declares that "wise people think before they act; fools don't and even brag about it."

Specialize in gaining connecting knowledge because it always pulls you out of confusion. Connecting knowledge is the analysis which considers how one action influences the next. It sees how tidbits of knowledge are intertwined and form a sequence which delivers you to a promising place. Comparable to a rock climber searching for the next crevice or protrusion where he can attach and advance himself, this type of know-how links where you are to where you want to be.

There is rock solid mobility of going from stable point to stable point. What is the grand advantage here? Connecting knowledge has an established reference point to future gains. You are thinking critically when the things you do bring you closer to the peace of God.

WHAT IS YOUR NEXT MOVE AND WHY?

Scenario: I'm going to smoke Bobby after school because he greatly disrespected me in front of several people. Where I'm from, when you get dissed, somebody has to go down in a blitz of bullets. Start writing Bobby's obituary because it's now needed. I know which way he goes home from school and can take him out with one shot. Nobody will know I did it. What are the consequences even if no one ever finds out I shot him? What if someone were preying on me right now and planning how they could leave me for dead without anyone knowing? What is the critical thinking man's next move? Seriously consider this critical thinking scenario because this decision could be critical to your freedom!! Definition of a bad bullet: six ounces closer to jail.

Explore even more:

1. An e-mail arrives from a guy who declares that you have just won a sweepstakes. The e-mail confirms your full name and current address as well as your last two employers. In order to lay claim to the money, all you need to do is confirm your bank account number. What will you do?

2. How do you determine where to get your car fixed?

3. Your friends are getting all the popular girls when they get high at parties. They give you an invite to a Thursday morning rave. What's your reply?

4. Your friend, who is a passenger in your car, dares you to double the speed limit around the curves. Challenging your manhood, she continues to dare you and will not shut up about it.

5. There is an elderly lady who runs a vending stand. Everyone adores her and it is known that she is raking in a few hundred dollars daily from her sales. Since you've been out of work for a while, you get the notion to take some of her earnings. How do you respond to that notion?

6. We live just a few miles from an International Airport. One day while pumping gas locally, an Italian-looking guy pulls next to me and asks if I'd like to get $2,000 worth of authentic Italian leather coats for $500 in cash. He says, "I've got to catch a flight to Italy in two hours. Give me the money and you can have the jackets."

8. You get a text message about organ enhancement—this is not about upgrading a musical instrument at your church. How do you respond to this text message?

Question: Are you making decisions based on values or circumstances?

There's a choice you make in everything you do, but in the end it's the choice you make that will certainly make you. Victories are thought out before they are fought out. Dozens of stations have talk shows. How often do you see a 'think show'? Talking is provocative, but thinking is imperative.

My late cousin, Damion was a DJ in the Miami, FL area. Although he was just a couple of years older than me, we shared some unforgettable memories. On one occasion, we were set to hang out in the city. He drove a mid-size Cadillac in which the entire back seat had been replaced by a bass speaker. Before we got into the car he said to me, "Cuz, I don't like to hear my music; I like to feel it!" Before I could slam the passenger door shut, the volume of the music blaring through the speakers made conversation impossible. Vibrations from the woofer caused the back of my seat to pulsate. That tremor-filled trip serves as a metaphor for the thinking man. Call to memory a beat or tune that causes you to bounce. Your robust thoughts ought to have such a vibe, vigor and gusto that you can feel them. Carried further, they parlay into a confident bounce, dance or swag that is evident to others.

CHAPTER NINE

A THINKING MAN'S GAME (2ND HALF)

———— CHECK OUT THIS CHAPTER————

Creators turn ordinary moments into memorable moments by creating what did not exist a moment ago.

It is important to think creatively because creativity is the engine that moves family, community, and society forward.

It is important to think correctly so that you are equipped to make proper decisions.

It is important to think constantly because you are being tested constantly.

If you do not control your own thoughts, be sure that you will not control anything else.

There's more to your life than how you are feeling at this moment.

Arise, let us go from here. (John 14:31b) NKJV

One of my all-time favorite childhood games was called Hungry Hungry Hippos. As a child, I had no idea that this silly and fun game was spoon-feeding me a bit of life wisdom. In this quick reflex, high-volume, action-packed game, up to four players use a plastic 'Hippo Mouth' to gobble marbles on the board. The object of this contest is to gobble more marbles than your opponent. Our version of the game involved lots of screaming and yelling as a means of expressing excitement while trying to distract the competition. Every Thanksgiving my cousins would come by, we would set up the game, begin gobbling marbles and work ourselves into a frenzy. On those occasions when I won, one of my cousins claimed that I cheated by tilting the table on which the game sat so that the marbles would all drift toward my hippo. I will not respond to this accusation; however the truth is, I did want to win every time I took to the hippo controls.

From the hallowed halls of the game, Hungry Hungry Hippos comes the wisdom found here in "Thinking Man's Game 2nd half." Tilt the table of life in your favor so that good things continually flow in your direction. This chapter aligns the reader for a Psalm 103:5 (NLT)—type life: "He fills my life with good things." In any closely contested athletic match, the team that tilts the second half of the game in their favor usually wins!

ARE YOU THINKING CREATIVELY?

Like a crafty point guard, this question breaks down the defense in the Thinking Man's Game. It is important to think creatively because creativity is the engine that moves family, community, and society forward. Everything man creates begins in the form of an inspired thought. Only a select few of us will ever visit outer space. Even if you are not among those chosen, there is enough untapped inner space between your ears for you to become a pioneer. Some of the galaxy's most imaginative ideas were birthed during the Era of Slavery. Have you ever heard the story of Henry 'Box' Brown? After thirty-three years of slavery, he escaped to freedom by having himself mailed to the abolitionists in Philadelphia. On the outside of that box was written "this side up" and "handle with care." What a flagship example of ingenious thinking! Metaphor alert, the only time the reader should allow himself to be boxed in is when it will result in a greater dimension of freedom.

Twenty four hours a day, God pours out creative notions to the receptive mind. The Heavenly Creator has endowed you with a mind so marvelous that even the best attempts to replicate it fall woefully short. Creative thinking is fun thinking! As a college sophomore, I tutored a motley crew of High School math students through a program called Upward Bound. Because of inner city blight, many of the students in that class were not issued text books. I felt obliged to bridge the gap between the urban teen apathetic about arithmetic and those thirsty to learn. I had to generate creative and enthusiastic ways to infuse math into their lives. One of my students used to say, "Mr. Eric, you make me think so hard that my brain hurts!" That momentary pain was the necessary elixir to help improve marginal grades in her math class. Creativity helped to engender math aptitude in a class where scholastic indifference was rampant.

The absence of creative thinking is glaring! In an acute way, non-creative thinking takes the form of jealousy. The epitome of non-creative thinking occurred during Operation Wall Street, when envious non-producers sought to impede and uproot the progress of those in the corporate banking industry. More commonly, non-creativity creeps into our conversations through statements like "Nothing going on but the same old, same old." Creative thinking in fact, offers relief from humdrum living.

In athletics, there are at least three realms of creativity as it relates to every sport. If you are gifted and hustle more than most, you will dominate your competition on the playing field. That's the first level. Once you develop an aptitude for the game and can convey it to the other players, you will at this level of creativity, master your competition from the coaching ranks. As quiet as it's kept, the highest plane of creativity occurs in the owner's box, where percentages are made from concessions, season ticket holders, television contracts and municipal contracts. Whichever realm you choose, I encourage you to stay forever creative.

Innovators improve life. Have you ever seen a 'creator' on the basketball court? What about the creator in the kitchen? Don't forget the creator in the graphic arts field. While some wait for things to happen and others wonder what is happening, the creator *makes* things happen. Creators turn ordinary moments into memorable moments by creating what did not exist a moment ago. Perhaps the most tremendous by-product of creative thinking is that it will likely outlive the thinker. No more woefully limited living because of decrepit thoughts! Bust loose with creative thinking!!

Creative thinking scenario—for a full month, dare to think creatively in some unchartered field. When you attend class, don't let the instructor do all the thinking for you. Persist until you can write down in black and white some idea you have nurtured. Who, reading these words will become a mental Matthew Henson; discovering thoughts where others are reluctant to travel? Exciting, productive notions are forming in your brain right now; as told by William Danforth, author of *I Dare You*. Where is it written that engines must have gasoline? Who established that a watch has to rest on the wrist? The prospects for the creative thinker are stupendous!

Are you thinking correctly? This is the question that will block out the crowd noise and help you remain focused during crunch time in the Thinking Man's Game. It is important to think correctly so that you are equipped to make proper decisions. Romans 12:2 (NIV) says it best: "Do not conform any longer to the pattern of this world, but be transformed by the renewing of your mind. Then you will be able to test and approve what God's will is— His good, pleasing and perfect will." You are the ancestor of a generation yet to exist. Correct thinking marinates in thoughts, activities and behaviors which enhance life for you now and for ensuing generations. Correct thinking keeps its audience on the path to a beneficial place.

Soon after I moved into my first apartment, I was introduced to Chris. Chris was perhaps the most compelling man of character I've met. He had a God-family-business paradigm which challenged me like never before. He had an unceasing, uncanny ability to quote books, the Bible and influential people. This occurred at a time when I commenced the adult responsibilities of paying my own bills and working my first job away from home. As I verified the things he said, it became obvious that he was a correct thinker. I also observed the way his wife and family responded to his remarkable leadership. He operated from a mode of correct thinking I sought to emulate.

People who do not think correctly attract too many problems. In contrast to correct thinking, corrupted thinking causes people to behave in ways that do not include God or consider the consequences which He set in motion long before we arrived. Two of America's young and popular talents paid the ultimate price for poor decisions. Actor John Belushi and college basketball player Len Bias both travelled that same treacherous trail. Incorrectly they believed that the 'high' given by cocaine would not have dire after-effects. Not recognizing the grave possibilities, they both died of drug overdoses. Correct thinking could have forestalled these tragedies.

Incorrect thinking equates to autonomous human reasoning. It always embraces the current thought process or suppositions, giving it a faddish appeal. It has the eerie affect as described in the book, Crime and Punishment where the author declares that, "Man can get used to anything." If that is true, I pray that you never accept average and mediocre; they are bereft of correct thinking.

Scenario: Do you ever feel so isolated, defeated and depressed that you've considered suicide? You've turned a moment of torment into an idol that has more value than the future God has orchestrated for you. This disappointing moment could never be more powerful than the God who's in every moment. Don't quit on life based on the assumption that it will only get worse. Stop and think correctly! There is more to this life than how you are feeling at this moment.

How would you counsel a friend who's in this scenario? Write out another example of incorrect thinking? How could it be corrected?

Are you thinking constantly? This question represents the game-winning shot for the "Thinking Man's Game."

It is important to think constantly because you are being tested constantly. Constant thinking strengthens the cord connecting present day activity with future expectations. Phillipians 4:8 (NIV)states, "Finally, brothers, whatever is true, whatever is noble, whatever is right, whatever is pure, whatever is lovely, whatever is admirable—if anything is excellent or praiseworthy—think about such things."

Whenever the stream of consistent thinking is interrupted, the future is forsaken. Social, economic, and agricultural imprudence contributed to the fall of the Roman Empire. History shows that a people who cannot or will not think constantly, will thirst for regulations and governing bodies to establish programs and policies for them. Ironically, not long after the establishment of these programs and policies, the very same people will complain, whine and protest about them. It's vital to constantly evaluate the policies, programs and pabulum placed before you by public officials. Cut back on constant thinking and you can expect your freedoms to fade.

Constant thinking centers on being strategically fruitful. In a Sunday evening session with perennial playoff powerhouse, the Oakton Cougar football team, I posed a series of questions to them to help construct a vision of manhood. I used the analogy of a football game which was divided into quarters. Here are just a few of the queries: The Kickoff question was-what is the one thing that you do better than anyone you know? First quarter: What is your educational game plan? What are you willing to do for professional development? Second quarter: What would you like your family life to look like? Where do you plan to go when a crisis hits? What will you do with your money? Third quarter: How will you bond with other people? Fourth quarter: What legacy do you want to leave?

If we do not think constantly, the mind will team up with the mouth and lead us to a mess. Do you know anyone who thinks constantly, then puts those upright thoughts in motion?

The enemy of your soul plays for keeps. Whatever he can do to keep you from thinking, he will do. He wants you to think as a 'thermometer' instead of a 'thermostat'. A thermometer reacts to its environment whereas a thermostat connects to a furnace or air conditioner to control the temperature of the environment. Thermometer thinkers harbor hopelessness because they can't control every day thoughts. In times of hopelessness, realize that there's more to your life than how you are feeling at this moment. A man who is hopeless for extended periods of time soon wants others to feel his plight. Fed enough faddish ideas, those who use a thermometer approach will adopt trends over truth, subjecting themselves to all forms of peer pressure. If we react to the truth more than we respond to the truth, the truth will irritate us.

A thermostat thinker exerts control over his environment. He seeks reliable and trusted sources of information before forming opinions. If you do not control your own thoughts, be sure that you will not control anything else. Attention, thermostat thinker! The condition of your surroundings should be improved because you have been changed for the better.

Questions: What occupies your mind? Do you know anyone who thinks things through? What happens when you don't think, think correctly, think constantly, think clearly, and think creatively?

No man is ever whipped until he quits thinking clearly, critically, creatively, correctly and constantly. These are the tools of a complete thinker, yet another hallmark of manhood. Since life leans in the direction of your dominant thoughts, ask God to help establish your thoughts and see life as He sees it.

CHAPTER TEN

MANGOES IN
THE PRODUCE AISLE

─────── **CHECK OUT THIS CHAPTER** ───────

Until you move out of your childhood home,
you are like the kid who can in fact ride a
bike—with the assistance of training wheels.

Jobs are practical, but they only
exercise a few of your abilities.

Careers are vital and they help
unlock your capabilities.

Callings are crucial—they unleash
your 'promotability'.

───────────────────────

You are the answer to someone's prayer and the solution to someone's problem!

Before graduating from college, I could not wait to move out of my parent's house! The slightest notion of moving out and moving on caused my heart to flutter with eager anticipation and welcome uncertainty. After gradu-ation, things did not go exactly as I had wanted. For six months following graduation, I lived in my parent's home in Henrico County, VA. During this time I worked on temporary assignments and as a substitute teacher in the city of Richmond. While I lived in my parents' home, I was required to remit one-third of my paycheck to them in order to cover room and board. At the time, I thought it was harsh treatment for dad to require such a chunk from my puny paycheck. My goal was to save money so that I could move out. His goal was to simulate real-life conditions so that I could move out faster. Knowing how best to motivate me, Dad collected rent from me in order to accelerate my move out of the house.

When I first returned home, I knew that living with my parents would be a short-lived proposition. For 20+ years, they had prepared me for this move-out moment. As a kid, I mostly observed and respected their rules. The same house rules that were designed to instill responsibility in me as a child also restricted my ability to blossom as a man; there-fore, I decided that it was time to ramp up the job search so I could move out! The time had come for me to spread my wings and embrace the charge to become a man. Glory hallelujah!!

That same path is available for you. After you've completely moved out, then you can fully move in to the productivity of manhood. Yes, there are some situations that dictate the need to stay at home for an additional period of time. If you are not sure whether that describes your circumstance, just ask your parent/guardian. If you are not yet ready, get ready! Until you move out of your childhood home, you are like the kid who can in fact ride a bike—with the assistance of training wheels! Unless that kid realizes that the training wheels are holding him up, he really thinks that he can ride a bike. Likewise, the man who remains in the 'parental sphere' deep into his twenties, thirties, forties and fifties has only a propped-up productivity. In some cases, the time to leave is clearly indicated. For instance, my wife and her brothers were all given a set of luggage by their parents as a gift for their 18th birthday. This was a definite indicator that it was time to leave the nest.

Moving out on your own seems more difficult than ever before, though. Economic, demographic and social factors will greet and grab you as soon as you decide to leave home. Without question, life is tough; I contend you are tougher. Similar to the fruit you find in the produce section which is bruised, rotten, and bitter; as you go down the 'Produce Aisle', you will encounter bumps, obstacles and hostilities.

You will be just fine as long as you realize that in each adversity, there is a seed of equal or greater benefit.

Everyone who has persevered through the previous nine chapters of this book has the fortitude necessary to successfully move out and stay out of his parents' house. Typically the number one catalyst for moving out is getting or having a job. Oh, what a joyous time it is when a young man acquires a job and moves out on his own! Being "on your own" is a big step—a necessary one for those who are "Onward to ManHood."

For the remainder of your productive life, you are preparing for one of three levels of living: a job, a career or a calling. These three levels can overlap or be mutually exclusive. You are about to embark upon the voyage of the Quad 4 man—brace yourself.

JOBS, THE FRINGES OF PRODUCTIVITY

Jobs are a man's initial and simplest form of productivity for which he can get paid. They represent general work, designed for workers to *use just a few of their abilities*. In a job, it's vital to establish a work ethic which will allow you to master the opportunities it presents. As an employee you are literally a 'usee', suitable to execute the commands of a boss who has more interest in the job you do than the person you become. A large portion of the workforce subsists at this level, locked into robotic existence. Have you ever heard someone say "I'm just happy to have a j-o-b?" That's the attitude of someone relegated to basic living who can only focus on personal needs versus the needs of others. Treat this assignment as a temporary holding station or a stepping stone to a greater responsibility. When we become fearful of losing the 'security blanket' provided by a job, our ambitions are slowly snuffed out. Jobs are practical but they only exercise a few of your abilities.

Making an honest living is commendable, and there is a dire need to get more boys and men to this fundamental level of living. This however, can become a default level of living. Sometimes we take a lackadaisical attitude about our work. We offer a half-baked effort to a boss, thinking it's enough; rationalizing by saying or thinking "Why should I care about the kind of performance I give him?" Perhaps, we think, "Hey it's just a job, a job that's not that important to me." Early in my Quad 4 experience, I tasted the fruit of mediocrity as my job journey floundered along the path of Temp work, substitute teaching, and shift work. For some inexplicable reason, I thought that was a great line-up. At that moment, I was in danger of being forever enclosed in the job to job cycle.

Thankfully, I received insight from key men, and I came to understand that I desperately needed an exit strategy. Without an exit strategy, we default to an exist strategy. Plan a mediocrity exit!

In every job, there are qualities which will serve you well. My first job allowed me to work on the campus of the University of Virginia as a Summer Camp Counselor. I served as a van driver, academic teacher, athletic instructor, resident assistant and even DJ. It was there I learned to appreciate the cultural diversity where Whites, Asians, and Indians all lived together.

As a' Sandwich Artist' for a national sub shop, I learned modesty and inventiveness when I was required to clean out the toilet at closing times— without any gloves. On one occasion, the commode was backed up with brown stuff. Seeing a box containing plastic sub 'sleeves', I took about four of them, put them inside of each other, covered my hand and arm up to my bicep, then proceeded to dive my protected arm into that indescribably nauseating lumpy brown soup! There's no way I thought that moment would give me the pay-it-forward value of humility and resourcefulness. Each time I left a job, I thanked God for the 'promotion', perceiving that the next position would be greater than the previous one.

While you are working at the job level, you will encounter numerous irritations. That's because, when you run somebody else's race you will regularly feel stymied and frustrated. Still, the conscientious employee can use each irritation as motivation for advancement. The well-known sports channel, ESPN, has a theme tune they play whenever an athlete makes a spectacular play. It's known as "da-da-da, da-da-da." Regardless of the sport highlighted, when that tune is queued up, it is guaranteed to be an impressive moment! I can assure you, no matter what kind of job you have, if you can create and string together enough "da-da-da, da-da-da" moments in your job, you are headed for your next level of brilliance!

CAREERS—PRODUCTIVITY WORKING FOR YOU

After you have mastered, using just a few of your abilities in a job, you are now ready to begin a career. Careers are vital; they help unlock your capabilities. Through specific responsibilities they provide daily occasions to blossom and make contributions beyond your cubicle. Your most valuable assets will remain latent until they are tested extensively. I remember working a fifteen-hour-day while in an engineering co-op during my sophomore year of college. That extended day involved reading, interpreting and organizing nuclear blue prints and regulations for a major utility company in Virginia. It turned out, that this was the paperwork that none of the full-time engineers wanted to do because of its tedium. That occasion taught me that someone with a job and a career can hold the same position; the main difference is in how they leverage time and expertise. While the job worker often supplies quick fixes and simple answers, a career worker deals in solutions.

Two great questions to answer in regard to your career—who are the people that repeatedly benefit from my career and what problems do I solve for them? Focusing on those people will help preserve the freshness and innovation of your career. One of my friends who owns an IT contracting firm calls his team a group of "solution ambassadors." He realizes that inventions and innovations are by products of eliminated problems. Every day we benefit from at least a dozen solutions. Already today we have profited from the light bulb, toothpaste, traffic light, transportation, housing, prepared meals, clothing, running water, etc. There is no cap on problems encountered or solutions needed. Fifteen years ago there was no such thing as speeding ticket insurance, an I-pod, wi-fi, streetball, Viagra, the organic food industry or female presidential candidates. It is ridiculous to think that there is not a solution to a problem!

Problems are precise so solutions have to be specific. There is no way to solve an abstract problem. Resting inside of you are answers to questions and solutions to problems. In a real sense you too are an answer to someone's prayer. Make a career of providing solutions. This is the stage of solidified productivity.

Grade school, trade school, college and military stints are golden chances to uncover your gifts so that your transition out of the house is more reasonable and less radical. While in the grade school stage of life, I was involved in basketball, football, track, band, French Club and Quiz Bowl. Each activity helped reveal a facet of my future necessary to cultivate a career. The majority of high school and college students are not aware of their true gifting. While you are in school, take time to locate and cultivate your talents so that when your formal schooling has ended you can utilize them in uncommon triumph. I realized that being effective means being selective.

I selected math and science as my topics of interest! I was told, by an engineer, that engineers make a lot of money, so I felt affirmed in that career selection. God made us with desires and goals to be accomplished. The late Tom Landry, who coached the Dallas Cowboys to two Super Bowl victories, described his role by saying, "My job as a coach is to make men do what they don't want to do so they can achieve what they always wanted to achieve." Jobs and careers are rife with things you don't want to do. The instructions gleaned from them have tremendous carry-over value. Through diligence, initiative and networking, you can turn even an ordinary job or career into a launch pad for a distinguished calling.

CALLING, POURING PRODUCTIVITY INTO OTHERS

Callings are deep-seated mental and spiritual desires to serve and inspire others. There is no cap on the service and inspiration which can emanate from a calling. In this zone, you master the art of eliminating the non-essential, enabling you to step away from average and launch into excellent advantage. Callings are God-sanctioned activities, which first percolate in your soul then, if cultivated, persist. It is the place where you can pour out your heart and soul and they come back energized. This type of mission lives through you and has such an inspirational swell that it continues to infuse others, even after you are dead. Callings, through customized work, are crucial for *unleashing your 'promotability.'* When shared, they cause others to be lifted.

There's no such thing as getting laid off or downsized from your calling. God's economy is unaffected by man's. Because that's true, there are two main considerations. First, you are the expression of the God who knows no boundaries. Second, your definite aim or purpose is actually a demonstration of His power working through you. Are you willing to unleash it? God does not take your gifts lightly; neither should you. Those gifts are constant reminders and previews of a gratified life. While you are cheering loudly for your favorite athlete, artist or entertainer, your calling reminds you that you too have a talent that can fill or impact stadiums filled with people. It reminds you that you were not created just to watch television but to fulfill a vision.

There's nothing automatic about it. A four-fold progression precedes high levels of productivity: good, rehearsed, creative, and accomplished. Interview anyone who is accomplished at what they do, and you will inevitably find that they followed a course similar to what was just described. The 'accomplished' level often puts you in position to be recognized and well-compensated. Compensation and recognition inundate the thoughts of young men but are not the end result of a calling. So many youths, who have ultimate dreams of playing professional sports, see it as the only way to 'make it'. When former NFL All-Pro running back Tiki Barber mused on his future beyond football, he said, "Sometimes you find a calling greater than the NFL." Here was a superbly talented athlete on top of his game, realizing that there is more excellence beyond the gridiron. What could be more meaningful than compensation, accolades and acknowledgment? Realizing the ultimate goal of a calling—you were created to serve and join God!

While the career man seeks to find his place on the organization chart, the called man seeks to find his place in God's kingdom. The farther you are from your calling, the more distress-filled life will be. Without an actual cause, boys and men will feign one, usually through some form of escapism such as virtual reality. I encourage every reader to delve into your calling. Someone on the other end of the hotline is waiting for you to answer. Someone answered your call; now it's time to answer a call. As a former math-instructor, I'm obligated to give you at least one formula: Whose you are + who you are = what you are to do. Discovering your Maker and your make-up certifies your meaning.

Will you join the ranks of the called or just admire them from a distance? I'm reminded of Pastor Paul Nichols, who was a prime example of a man in tune with his calling. In a section of Richmond, Virginia known as Church Hill, he headed a church, soup kitchen, and coat closet. That part of town was starved for a good example. Although Pastor Nichols passed away in 1990, his brand of Christian modelling and outreach reverberated throughout the city and ripples to this day. In a sense, he was the prototypical man going down the "Produce aisle."

To transform from job to career to calling requires major change. That change will take you by the throat until you take it by the hand. Man-go ahead and take those first steps down the produce aisle! Your first steps don't have to be blockbuster, just taken! Settling for anything short of a calling is captivity. Since productivity is another hallmark of manhood, you have three charges. Get a job and master it, identify a career and blossom in it, and discern your calling and flourish in it.

CHAPTER ELEVEN

FINAL MANDATE

I f significant men don't show up, we are bound for devastation.

When my son and daughter got their first bicycles, they discovered that bikes are a great source of fun, exercise, and responsibility. As novice bike riders, there are three primary things they learned to do. First, they learned to pedal continuously; second, keep their eyes on the pavement, and third, they learned to steer. It is a breeze to do any one of the three individually but coordinating all three requires practice. It can even generate some frustration along the way.

As their father, I also have three related responsibilities. First, I provide instruction, second, I look out for their wellbeing, and third, I speak encouraging words. Because I'm a seasoned bike rider, I can provide all the necessary tips for a successful bike ride. The more they embrace my instructions, the more they will master the ride.

Since the beginning of time, God has been doing the same for us. He has provided instruction, looked out for our well-being, and spoken encouraging words. He does this like none other and has been doing it so well for so long that we often take it for granted and don't realize He's doing it.

Life, just like a good bike, has gears. Gears are necessary to accommodate different speeds and changing terrains. Three gears of manhood are knowledge, wisdom, and understanding. These three cogs are vital to your livelihood and the likelihood that you will become significant.

Here we shift into the first gear, knowledge. Knowledge is information arranged in a beneficial way; it is necessary for accomplishment. Wisdom is the skillful leverage of knowledge and is necessary for establishment. Knowledge is necessary, while wisdom is crucial in becoming a prominent man. Understanding occurs when enough pieces come together to make sense of situations.

Rarely does the contemporary teaching approach tout the trio of wisdom, knowledge and understanding as the optimal approach to life. Do you know of a classroom where this is taught? Through the systematic and institutional eradication of biblical values, hope has shifted from the bedrock teachings of Jesus Christ to the ever-shifting sands of popular psychology and common core curriculums. What God acclaims, we hardly acknowledge. Information is hailed as the touchstone for forward progress. Problem resolution has been replaced with the euphoric panacea of feel good teaching. Hustle, bustle and activity saturation have eclipsed purpose.

KNOWLEDGE, THE LASTING ADVANTAGE

If we fail to promote knowledge, we will be manacled by ignorance. Neglecting knowledge results in the relentless and often fruitless chase for new information. With knowledge, men are the staples for their families and communities. They are also the pillars of church, business, government, and every significant realm. Without understanding, widespread abuse is inevitable. With it, men and their off-spring stand in the eternal favor of God. Neglected knowledge, forsaken wisdom, and absent understanding all preview a dried up soul. There's a quick way to distinguish between knowledge and wisdom. Knowledge is knowing that a tomato is a fruit. Wisdom is knowing not to put it in a fruit salad!

WISDOM IS SKILL IN MOTION

The soul of a man pines for the profound. Any man who wants to gain traction in the terrain of trying times must get upgraded with a 'Proverbs' package. It is the ultimate solution source for proactive and practical guidance in every major area of life including sex, money, relationships, self-esteem, achievement, success, drinking, parents, talking, life satisfaction, fulfillment, use of talents, etc. The power in the Proverbs occurs when the reader lives life by revelation versus experimentation.

King Solomon, the author of Proverbs, was a man of epic knowledge, wisdom and understanding. Even as king, he served us by collecting and sharing information and insight from every corner of life. Solomon's life reminds us that no matter what height you climb, you can be solid, successful and significant. Whatever situation we face, there is a parallel in the book of Proverbs. As long as wisdom is forsaken, foolishness will envelop us.

Sir Issac Newton said, "If I have seen farther than others, it is because I have stood on the shoulders of giants." There are at least thirteen colossal men who have lived out the Proverbs before me. Meriman Elliott, Virgil Tyler, Pastor Paul Nichols, Pastor Lloyd Linton, Marvin Kelley, George Wright, Chris Cherest, Evangelist Dr. Christipher

Joy, Elder Rudy Wiggins, Apostle Enoch Butler, Pastor Walter Hamilton, Pastor Lance Watson and Pastor Chester Mitchell. Each of these 'menfluential' persons has added a measure of excellence to my life and their communities. Because of their examples, I know we can reverse the trend of trifling men. If you thirst for correct personal leadership, you will find it, and then you can quench others with that same practical example.

UNDERSTANDING, A MODERN DAY SUPERPOWER.

How often have you wished that you could turn back the hands of time and relive a situation or make different choices? If you find a way to do that, get in touch with me—I want in! An alternative is to turn forward the hands of time and get a glimpse of the future so that you can act today based on that enlightened information. Since that option is available only to those who have time machines, let's explore the second best option. That is to get supreme knowledge, wisdom and understanding from God. Of the three, understanding is life's ultimate advantage! It gives its owner a pseudo-super power. Equipped with understanding, it's almost as if you are able to pause time, step out of the moment, fast forward to the end, and then act according to end-knowledge.

Freeze! Perhaps this is your first time hearing about the 'superpower' of understanding. If it is, use it immediately! If it's not, use it immediately! Here's how. Produce an inventory of how you spent your time, money and mental efforts this past week. These are likely your established patterns. Break the list into morning, afternoon and evening blocks. As completely as you can, itemize every idea, pursuit and expenditure. Fast forward to the likely ending of each and determine its conclusion. If course corrections need to be made, implement them now. If you are on track, better days are certain!

When my son and I first started reading comic books together, his favorite question to ask was, "Dad, who's gonna save the day?" With understanding, *you're* gonna save the day!

Project ahead to the end of your life. What do you think will be important to you in your final hours? Answer: Who you loved, who loved you, and what you did in the service of the Lord. In the end, it won't matter who had the shiniest rims, fattest paycheck, best 'yo' mamma jokes, most tattoos, sweetest record deal, biggest biceps, or woman with the biggest breasts. These things *seem* important because they are recognized and publicized as popular by people who want you to purchase their products. It's worth mentioning that today's choices are connected to tomorrow's consequences.

There are two possible paths which men take to their tomorrows. The pathway of hardship involves repeated misunderstanding and its travelers are confined by consequences. The path of nobility is laden with understanding and its travelers flourish in every domain imaginable.

Life is truly valuable; spend time improving its quality. You are not a cosmic happenstance that evolved from some organism wiggling in primordial ooze. Rather, you are an intended creation with divine design and a definite purpose. The misguided intellectuals and enthusiastic atheists will tell you God is irrelevant, disinterested, stuck, non-existent or dead. You cannot explain God until you've experienced God. Even then, it's tough to explain that which is beyond infinity. When you've truly experienced Him, you're inclined to exalt Him. Build some daily history with God so that when the stress of Quadrants 1-4 hits, your default response copycats that of Jesus Christ. For the man with no foundation, when times change a little, his life swoons a lot.

Your stability in life grows in direct proportion to your grip on God's word. Your peace in life grows in direct proportion to your grip on God's word. Your love in life grows in direct proportion to your grip on God's word. There are at least two reasons that God saves us. God saves us because we are worth saving and so that we might cause others to be saved. Jesus is the only one in all of eternity who was divinity wrapped in humanity. Religion comes in many names, but there is only one name by which men can be saved—that name is Jesus! My greatest hope for you is that after this life is over, you will be there on the other side with Him! If you don't make a reservation here in this life, it'll be too late when it's over.

I started to embrace these truths in the summer of '85. It was then that I spent part of that summer at a camp in Charlottesville, VA. My favorite things to do were play basketball, eat and make people laugh. Strong profanity was a major part of my comedic repertoire. I could curse effortlessly and well enough to make a sailor from the ghetto blush! So raunchy was my language that, Tiffany, my buddy from that camp, recognized me for being as funny as Eddie Murphy. At that time, his humor was raw, uncut, and vulgar. I smiled when I read her assessment in my autograph book, but on the inside, I knew that it meant being known for my expletives rather than my character. Perhaps those expletives *were* the expression of my character. At any rate, that was an eye-opening moment. From that day forward, I vowed to change. I knew I couldn't be sinless, but I could sin less.

This is more than a book; it's an at-home personal workshop—meant to be read, absorbed, applied and actualized. I believe this message will send forth spiritual awakening and renewal in tens of thousands of people all over the globe. While there are hordes of overzealous prosecutors, eager to throw the book *at you*, I am eager to get the contents of this book *in you*. A man or woman infused with this type of meaning will soar from mundane and marginal living to abundant life. They will topple ungodly influences and spread the truth far and wide because they are defined by Divine design. You could be hurled into eternity at any moment. In your hands are the guidelines for establishing lasting, Godly masculinity. Manhood is an invisible power with visible privileges. You have read about the privileges, now exercise the power.

ERIC ELLIOTT: this Richmond, Virginia Native is a graduate of Old Dominion University who went on to thrive in the world of Software Test Engineering. Although he has a technical background, he is firmly entrenched in manhood as a husband, father, son, brother, teacher, friend, impact speaker, and author. From each of those platforms, he's extended timeless encouragement to numerous friends and associates.

Over time God has established Eric as an accomplished, creative, eye-opening and mind-renewing speaker. As a presenter he has uplifted schools, teams, churches and organizations throughout the Mid-Atlantic region. Audiences have included Christ Fellowship Church, Herndon Middle School, J. Sargeant Reynolds Community College Public Speaking Class, Good Shepherd Baptist Church, 21st Street Church of God, the National Society of Black Engineers (NSBE), the Oakton Cougar Football Team, the residents of White Oak Correctional Facility, the Virginia Women's Correctional Center, the North Richmond YMCA, Old Dominion University Upward Bound Program, Virginia Union University Toast Masters and Wooster College student body.

This book is the overflow of his determination to strengthen souls. It connects the heart of the reader to the gusto of the gospel of Jesus Christ. With it, he can now reach out to hundreds of thousand he could not otherwise reach.

Visit www.EricJElliott.com for products, services and bookings.

Made in the USA
Middletown, DE
04 June 2015